Mrs BEETON'S

TRADITIONAL CAKE DECORATING

Mrs BEETON'S

TRADITIONAL CAKE DECORATING

Consultant Editor   **Bridget Jones**

WARD LOCK

This paperback edition published 1993
First published 1991 by Ward Lock
Villiers House, 41/47 Strand, London WC2N 5JE,
England

A Cassell imprint

Printed and bound in Great Britain by
The Bath Press, Avon

British Library Cataloguing in Publication Data
Beeton, Mrs. *1836–1865*
    Mrs. Beeton's traditional cake decorating.
    1. Cakes, Decoration
    I. Title
    641.8653

    ISBN 0 7063 7173 9

**Mrs Beeton's is a registered
trademark of Ward Lock Ltd**

CONTENTS

INTRODUCTION

The art of creating beautifully decorated cakes is now at everyone's fingertips – the only essential qualification is enthusiasm. As with many other culinary skills, cake decorating has been simplified over the past decade with the introduction of labour-saving ingredients, icings and utensils. You certainly do not have to be a professional to achieve excellent results.

Perhaps the greatest revolution has been in the availability of sugar paste and moulding icings. This has produced a new style of decoration. The icing is simply rolled out and smoothed over the cake to give a softer line than was possible with royal icing. Sugar paste sets hard enough to decorate, it may also be moulded into shapes and flowers so that mastery of the icing bag is no longer a prerequisite for cake decorating.

Having tasted success the easy way, the enthusiast may advance to royal icing, run-outs, Garrett frills, collars and decorative flowers. This book is packed with information, instructions and ideas for everything from basic cakes decorated with buttercream to the more advanced decorations for the ultimate wedding cake.

USEFUL WEIGHTS AND MEASURES

USING METRIC OR IMPERIAL MEASURES

Throughout the book, all weights and measures are given first in metric, then in Imperial. For example 100 g/4 oz, 150 ml/¼ pint or 15 ml/1 tbsp.

When following any of the recipes use either metric or Imperial – do not combine the two sets of measures as they are not interchangeable.

EQUIVALENT METRIC/IMPERIAL MEASURES

Weights The following chart lists some of the metric/Imperial weights that are used in the recipes.

METRIC	IMPERIAL
15 g	½ oz
25 g	1 oz
50 g	2 oz
75 g	3 oz
100 g	4 oz
150 g	5 oz
175 g	6 oz
200 g	7 oz
225 g	8 oz
250 g	9 oz
275 g	10 oz
300 g	11 oz
350 g	12 oz
375 g	13 oz
400 g	14 oz
425 g	15 oz
450 g	16 oz
575 g	1¼ lb
675 g	1½ lb
800 g	1¾ lb
900 g	2 lb
1 kg	2¼ lb
1.4 kg	3 lb
1.6 kg	3½ lb
1.8 kg	4 lb
2.25 kg	5 lb

Liquid Measures The following chart lists some metric/Imperial equivalents for liquids. Millilitres (ml), litres and fluid ounces (fl oz) or pints are used throughout.

METRIC	IMPERIAL
50 ml	2 fl oz
125 ml	4 fl oz
150 ml	¼ pint
300 ml	½ pint
450 ml	¾ pint
600 ml	1 pint

Spoon Measures Both metric and Imperial equivalents are given for all spoon measures, expressed as millilitres and teaspoons (tsp) or tablespoons (tbsp).

All spoon measures refer to British and U.S. standard measuring spoons and the quantities given are always for level spoons.

Do **not** use ordinary kitchen cutlery instead of proper measuring spoons as they will hold quite different quantities.

METRIC	IMPERIAL
1.25 ml	¼ tsp
2.5 ml	½ tsp
5 ml	1 tsp
15 ml	1 tbsp

Length All linear measures are expressed in millimetres (mm), centimetres (cm) or metres (m) and inches or feet. The following list gives examples of typical conversions.

METRIC	IMPERIAL
5 mm	¼ inch
1 cm	½ inch
2.5 cm	1 inch
5 cm	2 inches
15 cm	6 inches
30 cm	12 inches (1 foot)

CUP CONVERSION CHART

50 ml	2 fl oz	¼ cup
125 ml	4 fl oz	½ cup
150 ml	¼ pint	⅔ cup
250 ml	8 fl oz	1 cup
300 ml	½ pint	1¼ cups
450 ml	¾ pint	1¾ cups
600 ml	1 pint	2½ cups

US EQUIVALENTS

UK	US
Plain or self-raising flour 100 g/4 oz	All-purpose flour 1 cup
Granulated sugar 100 g/4 oz	Granulated sugar ½ cup
Caster sugar 100 g/4 oz	Superfine sugar ½ cup
Icing sugar 100 g/4 oz	Confectioners' sugar ¾ cup
Butter or margarine 100 g/4 oz	¼ lb/½ cup
Plain chocolate 25 g/1 oz	Unsweetened chocolate 1 square
Chopped nuts 25 g/1 oz	¼ cup
Jam 225 g/8 oz	¾ cup
Currants, raisins, sultanas 100 g/4 oz	¾ cup
Citrus peel 100 g/4 oz	¾ cup
Glacé cherries 50 g/2 oz	⅓ cup
Double cream	Heavy cream
Single cream	Light cream
Cocktail stick	Toothpick
Piping bag	Pastry bag

It is important to follow the recipes closely for success. Use an accurate set of scales for weighing and a measuring jug for measuring quantities of fluid and standard spoon measures. For the U.S., use a 1-cup liquid measuring cup, which is also marked with smaller measures, for liquids. For dry ingredients, use a set of four graduated measuring cups, consisting of ¼-, ⅓-, ½- and 1-cup measures.

Weigh all the ingredients before you begin to prepare the mixture so that they are all ready to be added as they are needed. It is a good idea to weigh dry ingredients, such as flour and sugar, before softer foods, like butter and margarine, as this saves having to wash the scoop or container on the scales in between weighing the items. Keep the prepared ingredients separate until they are ready to be mixed in the right order.

OVEN TEMPERATURES

Whenever the oven is used, the required setting is given as three alternatives: degrees Celsius (°C), degrees Fahrenheit (°F) and gas.

The temperature settings given are for conventional ovens. If you have a fan oven, then read the notes below and follow the manufacturer's instructions.

°C	°F	gas
110	225	¼
120	250	½
140	275	1
150	300	2
160	325	3
180	350	4
190	375	5
200	400	6
220	425	7
230	450	8
240	475	9

NOTE ON FAN OVENS AND CONTINENTAL OVENS

All the temperatures and timings given are for a conventional oven, with main heating sources located on both sides (in addition, some electric ovens may have a low-powered element located in the base).

Forced convection ovens – or fan ovens – have a built-in fan which re-circulates the hot air, providing even temperatures over a greater number of shelves. This is ideal for batch baking. This type of oven heats up very quickly and food cooks more quickly. It is the equivalent of between 10 and 20 degrees hotter than the conventional cooker. When using this type of oven always follow the manufacturer's instructions closely and adjust the cooking temperatures accordingly.

Continental electric ovens have the heating elements located in the top and bottom of the oven. These do give slightly different results and the manufacturer's instructions should be followed closely.

MICROWAVE INFORMATION

Occasional microwave hints and instructions are included for certain recipes, as appropriate. The information given is for microwave ovens rated at 650-700 watts.

The following terms have been used for the microwave settings: High, Medium, Defrost and Low. For each setting, the power input is as follows: High = 100% power, Medium = 50% power, Defrost = 30% power and Low = 20% power.

All microwave notes and timings are for guidance only: always read and follow the manufacturer's instructions for your particular appliance. The aim in providing microwave information is to indicate which recipes can be cooked successfully by that method, or short cuts which can be made by using the microwave for a small part of the preparation of a recipe.

Always remember to avoid putting any metal in the microwave and never operate the microwave empty.

INGREDIENTS AND EQUIPMENT

The correct choice of ingredients and equipment lays the foundation for success when decorating cakes. Here you will find a wealth of useful information, from a list of simple, shop-bought cake decorations to the details of specialist equipment.

Like all crafts, cake decorating employs traditional tools and time-honoured methods, but today these exist in tandem with new products, ready-made to ease the burden on the busy cook. These commercial products do not necessarily demean the craft; indeed they frequently enable us to develop it further and increase our skills. This chapter lists, and briefly discusses, the main ingredients and items of equipment which are used for decorating cakes.

INGREDIENTS

ALMOND PASTE

Almond paste is believed to have originated in the Middle East and is made from ground almonds, eggs and sugar. It is used to cover rich fruit cakes to prevent the crumbs from discolouring the icing. It also provides a smooth, flat surface for the icing. Almond paste may also be moulded to make cake decorations. Home-made almond paste is usually made with a mixture of caster and icing sugar and has a slightly grainy texture.

APRICOT GLAZE

Apricot glaze is a smooth, clear syrup made from boiled, sieved apricot jam and is used as a glaze or brushed over fruit cakes before covering with almond paste. Any jam or marmalade of similar colour may be used.

BUTTER

Fresh butter gives a good flavour to buttercreams but it may need to be softened before use. Alternatively, use one of the butterfats mixed with vegetable oil for easy spreading. Whenever possible use unsalted butter for making icings.

CHOCOLATE

Dark plain, milk and white chocolate have a variety of uses in cake decorating. They may be used to make icings and coverings as well as decorations. Chocolate and chocolate work is discussed in detail in the chapter beginning on page 114.

CORNFLOUR

Cornflour is used as a dusting powder when modelling with sugar paste.

EGGS

Ensure that eggs are fresh and from a reputable source as they are used raw in cake decorating. Eggs should be stored in their container in the refrigerator. Before use they should be thoroughly washed and dried with absorbent kitchen paper. Separate eggs carefully and place the whites in a clean, greasefree bowl. Remove the stringy parts from the white and ensure that no yolk is present. Use whites for icing and yolks for rich buttercream and confectioners' custard.

EGG SUBSTITUTES

Dried egg white, albumen powder and albumen substitute are available from specialist cake decorating shops or sold under brand names in supermarkets. If stored in an airtight container in a cool, dry place dried egg white has a long shelf life. It is therefore a valuable storecupboard ingredient and eliminates the problem of what to do with the egg yolks. If used correctly, it gives excellent results in icings. It is either made up to a liquid or sifted dry with the icing sugar. Follow the package instructions.

FOOD COLOURINGS

Colourings are available as pastes, liquids or powders. Paste colours are strong and are recommended for sugar paste as they will not alter the consistency. Use the weaker liquid colours for royal icing, glacé icing and fondant. Use either with buttercreams. Powder colours tend to be a little messy. Except for gold and silver all colours are edible but will vary as to derivation. Pure natural colours tend to lack clarity but are sold in a limited range as are tartrazine-free colours. Read the labels for more information.

Compounds are also available. They are concentrated liquids that combine colouring and flavouring. Compounds should always be used sparingly.

FRESH CREAM

Not long ago, the choice of creams was limited to single or double, depending upon the butterfat content. Today, supermarkets offer a wide range of creams, including half fat cream, whipping cream, pre-whipped and aerosol creams, long life or frozen cream and 'alternative' creams which include a percentage of vegetable fats.

Cream should be kept in a cool place or refrigerator until ready to use. Check the 'sell' or 'use by' date, especially in warm weather. Use as a filling for cakes and gâteaux.

GLYCERINE

This is a thick, sweet, colourless liquid that helps to keep icing soft. It is available from chemists.

GROUND ALMONDS

Usually a mixture of bitter and sweet almonds. Use when as fresh as possible and store in a well-sealed container in a cool, dark place or in the refrigerator.

ICING SUGAR

Icing sugar is the basis for most icings, although granulated and caster sugar are both used in frostings. Icing sugar is usually sold in 450 g/1 lb packets but it is more economical to buy the 3 kg/6.6 lb bags from supermarkets. Store the sugar in a cool, dry place, re-sealing the bag after use. Alternatively, keep it in a large screw-topped jar. Most brands of icing sugar contain a moisture-absorbing substance to prevent the formation of lumps but for professional results when making royal icing always sift the sugar two or three times.

INSTANT ROYAL ICING

This commercial product is available from grocers and supermarkets. It is sold in 450 g/1 lb packets. Dried egg white and corn starch have been mixed with icing sugar and only water needs to be added. It is simple to use and makes very good royal icing. Good when only small amounts are required.

LIQUID GLUCOSE

Sometimes called glucose syrup, this is a clear tasteless syrup available from chemists and specialist shops. It is used to make sugar paste pliable. When measuring, warm the syrup first or use a hot, metal spoon and scrape away any excess underneath the spoon to ensure accurate measuring. Glucose syrup has a limited shelf life.

MARZIPAN

Marzipan usually refers to a commercial product that is made with icing sugar and liquid glucose. It is smoother and more pliable than almond paste and inexpensive brands are often coloured bright yellow. Use only white almond paste or marzipan under white icing.

PETAL PASTE

Petal paste is available in powder or paste form from specialist shops. It is used on its own for modelling flowers or may be added to sugar paste for decorations that need to set hard and strong. Store in a cool place (not a refrigerator). It has a limited shelf life.

PIPING GEL

A clear colourless flavourless jelly (usually coloured and flavoured for gâteaux), piping gel is mixed in very small quantities with royal icing for fine brushwork to prevent the icing from drying out too quickly. It is available from specialist shops.

PURE ALCOHOL

This usually means brandy, but other spirits may be used to brush over cakes or to stick sugar paste decorations on to dry icing. Cooled, boiled water may be used instead.

SUGAR PASTE

Also known as decorating icing or mallow paste, or sometimes referred to as fondant icing, this is used in the same way as almond paste. It may be rolled out to cover both fruit and sponge cakes and may also be moulded to make decorations. It is easy to use and gives a soft finish, both in texture and appearance. It may be home-made or is available by the 450 g/1 lb or in 5 kg/11 lb packs from specialist shops and some bakers. A ready-to-roll icing is available under a trade name from supermarkets and grocers. Sold in 227 g/8 oz packets, it is sweeter and softer in texture than sugar paste and should be kneaded with a little sifted icing sugar to a manageable consistency before use. Always keep sugar paste well wrapped to prevent it drying out.

DECORATIONS

All decorations on a cake should be edible unless they are large enough to be lifted off easily before cutting the cake; for example bride and groom, horseshoes, candles and holders, novelty characters. Small, inedible decorations could be harmful if swallowed.

SIMPLE DECORATIONS TO BUY

These may be readily purchased from grocers, supermarkets and sweet shops. A specialist cake-decorating shop will have a wider selection, especially as regards sugar flowers and other piped items. Avoid using strongly coloured decorations, as the colour tends to ooze when damp.

- angelica
- candy orange and lemon slices
- chocolate buttons (brown and white), chocolate chips, chocolate coffee beans, chocolate vermicelli, chocolate eggs, chocolate flakes and chocolate wafer mints
- coconut (shredded or desiccated)
- crystallised flowers and fruits
- crystallised pineapple
- crystallised violets and rose leaves
- dragees (silver and coloured shiny sugared balls)
- glacé cherries (red, green and yellow)
- jellies and jelly beans
- liquorice sweets, laces and comfits
- marshmallows
- pastilles
- piped sugar flowers
- sugar-coated chocolate beans
- sugar-coated cumin and mimosa balls
- sugar drops
- sugar strands
- sugared almonds
- strawberry and chocolate crunch

SIMPLE DECORATIONS TO MAKE

Instructions for making these will be found in the chapters that follow.

- chocolate, grated, piped, scrolled, leaves, used for dipping nuts, fruits and marzipan
- desiccated coconut, toasted or coloured
- marzipan – moulded into fruits, vegetables, leaves, characters
- nuts, toasted, halved, slivered, chopped, chocolate dipped, praline
- royal icing, piped into flowers, birds and various designs, also run-outs
- sugar, frosted flowers and leaves; coloured sugar
- sugar paste, moulded into shapes, characters or flowers; rolled out and cut into motifs and badges

EQUIPMENT

Having the right equipment can make all the difference to successful cake decorating, but the vast array of implements and utensils available in specialist shops can be bewildering. This chapter lists some of the more useful items.

It is important to keep cake decorating equipment away from general use, as all utensils must be clean and grease-free. Egg whites will not whisk up successfully if there is a trace of grease on bowl or whisk, and a sieve used previously for soup will flavour and colour the icing accordingly!

Ensure that all equipment is thoroughly rinsed and dried after use and stored in bags or containers away from dust, grease and kitchen steam. A fisherman's plastic tool box makes an excellent keeper for all the smaller items, such as paint brushes and nozzles.

BEATERS

Food mixers may be used for albumen-based icings but care should be taken that whisks are clean. Do not use a food processor. For whipping cream, use a small wire balloon whisk or, for large quantities, a hand-held electric whisk.

BOARD

An 18 × 25 cm/7 × 10 inch laminex board used with a laminex rolling pin will ensure paper-thin paste without sticking. Avoid cutting the surface with sharp knives and do not use for any other purpose.

BOWLS

When making icings or frostings, use un-cracked china or glass bowls. Metal bowls tend to discolour the icing and plastic ones are easily scratched. For whipping cream, use a large glass, china or aluminium bowl. Avoid plastic, as it is difficult to clean and may taint the cream.

CRIMPERS

Several designs are available for pressing designs into soft sugar paste. Similar effects may be achieved with a fork, potato peeler or butter curler.

ICING BAGS AND NOZZLES

For professional results, throw away the icing gun and use paper icing bags and good quality nozzles. **Paper icing bags** are available in various sizes from specialist shops or may be home-made (see page 18). **Nylon icing bags** should be used with savoy nozzles for piping buttercream. Wash and rinse well before drying thoroughly.

Choose good quality, smooth, seamless nozzles. Metal nozzles are better than plastic ones, since they give sharper definition. Always wash and dry each nozzle well after use and avoid distorting the pattern end. Do not buy any nozzles with ridges or collars that prevent them sitting neatly in the icing bag.

Each nozzle has a special function and is available in several sizes. Beginners are advised to select the medium sizes. The finer nozzles are for professional work and the large ones require considerable control of the icing. For some applications, left-handed nozzles are available. The table on page 19 shows how the various nozzles are best used. Please note, however, that because manufacturers differ in the number codes they allocate to nozzles, only writing nozzles may be identified by numbers.

MARZIPAN SPACERS

These are useful devices to ensure even rolling of marzipan or sugar paste. A good idea for those cooks who find it difficult to apply even pressure when rolling out.

MODELLER

This is similar to a potter's tool. It is usually double ended for smoothing, gouging out or marking a pattern.

PAINT BRUSHES

Use fine, good quality sable brushes that will not lose their hairs. Use with powder or liquid food colouring for brush embroidery, writing and fine art work. Wash and dry brushes carefully, making sure that all hairs are lying flat.

PALETTE KNIVES

A 10 cm/4 inch blade is ideal for icing the sides of cakes, while a larger 15 cm/6 inch blade is used for spreading icing over the top.

PAPERS

Greaseproof paper is available in rolls or sheets in various qualities. It is used for wrapping cakes, lining cake tins, making small icing bags and tracing patterns.

Non-stick baking parchment (silicone paper) is sold in rolls under various trade names. It is used in much the same way as greaseproof paper, but because it is stronger it is particularly suitable for making large icing bags. It may also be used for run-outs, piping flowers etc. It will not stick to adhesive tape and must be secured with pins.

Waxed paper is more expensive than either greaseproof or silicone. Available in rolls or sheets, it is excellent for large run-outs and when icing flowers, but is not suitable where heat is required. When using it for run-outs, choose the sheet form, as it is essential that the paper be flat and uncreased. It will not stick to adhesive tape – use pins instead.

PASTRY BRUSHES

Keep a wide, flat pastry brush for brushing away dry cake crumbs, and a second brush for applying glaze.

RIBBON INSERTION TOOL

Used for cutting slits in the icing when threading ribbon, this is a useful tool for anyone who regularly ices celebration cakes.

ROLLING PIN

A long, non-stick laminex rolling pin is best for rolling out large quantities of sugar paste, but these are expensive. Alternatively, use a china or new wooden rolling pin or wooden dowel. The latter must be dusted frequently with cornflour to prevent sticking. A 23 cm/9 inch laminex rolling pin is necessary for rolling sugar paste very thinly when making flowers or a frill.

RULER OR STRAIGHT EDGE

This is a stainless steel rigid rule for flat icing the top of a cake. A rigid, well-scrubbed wooden ruler may be used instead.

SCISSORS

A small pair of sharp pointed scissors will prove useful.

SCRAPER

Used for smoothing the icing on the sides of cakes. Buy a firm plastic or stainless steel scraper; avoid any that bend easily. Some have a serrated side for a decorative finish.

SIEVE

Buy a fine nylon mesh sieve, kept solely for sifting icing sugar. A metal sieve may taint or discolour the icing.

TURNTABLE

A turntable is invaluable for flat icing a round cake. Choose one that is well balanced and will not slide across the table. Turntables may be made from plastic, injection-moulded nylon or aluminium. Prices vary considerably. Buy the best quality that you can afford if your use will justify the cost.

WOODEN SPOONS

Buy new spoons in various sizes. A small batter paddle with a hole in the centre is useful when making royal icing.

USEFUL EXTRAS

Cutters Sets of sharp straight-edged and fluted cutters. Alternatively, cut around upturned saucers, lids, cups, etc.

Dummy Polystyrene artificial 'cake' in various sizes and shapes used to practise icing techniques. It is a good idea to secure the dummy to a heavy base with glue and/or nails through the base.

Flower nail Used for piping flowers. Alternatively, make your own by using a cork on the end of a short knitting needle or wooden meat skewer.

Glass-headed stainless steel pins For securing ribbon or marking positions.

Tweezers Useful for placing small decorations into position.

Wooden cocktail sticks (toothpicks) For piping roses (see page 102) and Garrett frill.

Wooden meat skewer Use blunt end rounded off when working with sugar paste.

FINISHING TOUCHES

BOARDS

Use deep drum boards for all fruit cakes and large gâteaux. The thinner boards are for lighter sponges and plaques. The boards are available in various shapes and sizes and should be at least 5 cm/2 inches larger than the cake. A 'universal' board may be used for either round or square cakes. The boards are covered in silver, gold or Christmas paper and only a specialist shop will stock the whole range. A limited supply of traditional round or square boards is available in most stationers, bakers and suppliers of artists' materials.

BOARD EDGES

Gilt or silver paper ribbon may be purchased to place around the edge of drum boards to give a professional finish.

ICING PENS

These resemble fine felt-tip pens and are used for direct art work on hard icing. They are particularly useful for adding details such as eyes.

PILLARS

Plastic or plaster pillars are used to separate the tiers of a cake. Available in white, gold or silver finish.

RIBBONS

Although most haberdashers will offer a range of ribbons you will probably find a greater selection at a specialist cake-decorating shop. Double-faced satin ribbon is sold in a variety of colours and widths ranging from 1.5 mm to 2·5 cm (⅟₁₆ – 1 inch) and wider. Single-faced ribbon may also be used. When matching ribbon to icing, remember that the icing tends to dry to a darker shade. Iron the ribbon, if necessary, before use and leave to cool before measuring and attaching to the cake.

SEQUIN RIBBON

These shiny sequinned bands make ideal substitutes for ribbon on gold, silver and ruby wedding aniversary cakes. Available from haberdashers.

SPARKLE OR LUSTRE

Fine coloured reflective powder which may be lightly dusted on to brush embroidery or flowers to add an effect. 'Sparkle' has larger reflective particles than 'Lustre'.

MAKING A PAPER ICING BAG

Use greaseproof paper, non-stick baking parchment (silicone paper) or waxed paper.

1 Cut a 20 cm/8 inch square piece of paper and cut it in half diagonally.

2 Position paper as shown in diagram and hold 'B' flat on to the table with your left hand. Take hold of 'A' in your right hand.

3 Fold 'A' round towards you until it meets 'B' to form a cone.

4 Hold 'A' and 'B' firmly in position with your right hand, positioning fingers on top and thumb underneath. Take hold of 'C' in your left hand.

5 Lift the cone off the table and wrap 'C' around the cone to meet 'B' at the back.

6 Points A, B and C should now be together.

7 Fold down points to secure the bag.

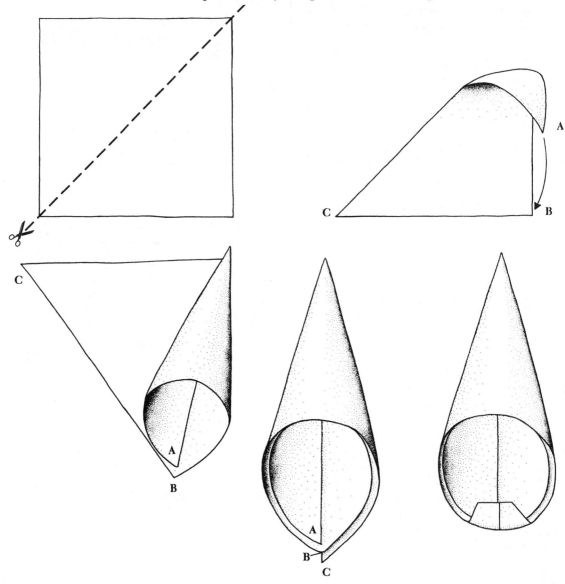

NOZZLES AND THEIR USES

NOZZLE	USE
'Writer" Plain Sizes 00, 0, 1, 2, 3, 4. (Select 0 and 1 for general use)	Writing, straight lines, line work, dots, beads, outline work, scribbles, lace and embroidery work
Shell	Edging cakes at base or around the top. Scrolls
Star Sizes 5, 6, 7, 8 and 9 for small coarse star; 11, 13 and 15 for large	Stars or simpler 'shell' effect for piping around the edge and base of the cake
Ribbon (size 22)	Basket weave
Petal	Piping flowers such as small roses
Leaf	Leaves or petals
Savoy Preferably metal with fine star 'teeth'	Piping buttercreams and softer icings

'Writer' Plain

Shell

Star

Ribbon

Petal

Leaf

Savoy

CAKE COVERINGS AND FILLINGS

Even a simple cake can be made extra special by adding a little icing, a golden glaze or a nutty topping. This chapter includes recipes to complement formal cakes as well as plain ones. In addition, a quick-reference chart provides a useful guide to selecting the right icing for the type of cake.

GLAZES AND COATINGS

Glazes are used to give a shiny coating to food. Pastry, cakes and biscuits may be glazed with egg white, egg wash, sugar syrup or warmed jam such as apricot glaze, and then covered with crumbs, ground nuts, coconut, marzipan, almond paste or praline. Fruit flans or tartlets are often coated with a sweet liquid thickened with arrowroot.

APRICOT GLAZE

Brush this glaze over a cake before applying the marzipan. Any yellow jam or marmalade may be used.

225 g/8 oz apricot jam

Warm the jam with 30 ml/2 tbsp water in a small saucepan over a low heat until the jam has melted. Sieve the mixture and return the glaze to the clean saucepan. Bring slowly to the boil. Allow to cool slightly before use.

SUFFICIENT TO COAT THE TOP AND SIDES OF ONE 20 CM/8 INCH CAKE

☀ **MICROWAVE TIP** Melt the jam with the water in a bowl on High. Sieve into a small basin and heat the syrup on High. Cool slightly before use.

CHOCOLATE GLAZE

A little oil gives this icing sugar glaze its shine. It may be poured over chocolate cakes or it can be used to coat plain sponge cakes to provide a contrast in flavour. Store any leftover glaze in an airtight container in the refrigerator.

100 g/4 oz plain chocolate, broken into
    small pieces
5 ml/1 tsp vegetable oil
25 g/1 oz caster sugar

Combine the chocolate, oil and caster sugar in a heatproof bowl. Stir in 45 ml/3 tbsp boiling water. Place the bowl over hot water and stir gently until the chocolate has melted. Remove from the heat and cool slightly before pouring the chocolate glaze over the cake.

SUFFICIENT TO COVER TOP AND SIDES OF ONE 18 CM/7 INCH CAKE

☀ **MICROWAVE TIP** Melt all the ingredients in a small bowl on Medium for 2-3 minutes.

MARASCHINO GLAZE

Unlike the apricot glaze, this one is based upon icing sugar, with milk and butter added to enhance the shiny effect.

30 ml/2 tbsp softened butter
175 g/6 oz icing sugar
30-45 ml/2-3 tbsp milk
5-10 ml/1-2 tsp maraschino liqueur or
    syrup from maraschino cherries
1-2 drops red food colouring (optional)

Put the butter into a bowl. Using a wooden spoon, gradually work in the icing sugar until thoroughly mixed. Bring the milk to the boil in a small saucepan and stir it into the mixture, with the liqueur or syrup. Add a couple of drops of colouring, if liked, to tint the icing a pale pink. The glaze should be thick enough to spread lightly, yet be able to trickle over the edge of a cake and drip down the sides.

SUFFICIENT TO COVER ONE 25 CM/10 INCH RING CAKE OR 24 SMALL CAKES

MRS BEETON'S TIP An icing sugar glaze of this kind may be used on top of an icing of a different colour and flavour. Maraschino glaze looks particularly good on chocolate icing.

GLAZE FOR SWEET FLANS

This slightly thickened glaze is useful for coating fresh or canned fruit as a decoration for light gâteaux. It can also be used with fresh fruit to top a plain cheesecake.

5 ml/1 tsp arrowroot
150 ml/¼ pint fruit syrup from canned or
    bottled fruit or 150 ml/¼ pint water
    and 25 g/1 oz sugar
1-3 drops food colouring
lemon juice

In a bowl, mix the arrowroot to a paste with a little of the cold fruit syrup or water. Pour the remaining syrup into a saucepan and bring to the boil. If using water, add the sugar and bring to the boil, stirring constantly until all the sugar has dissolved. Pour on to the arrowroot mixture, stir well, then return to the saucepan. Bring to the boil, stirring constantly. Add the appropriate food colouring, then stir in lemon juice to taste. Use at once.

SUFFICIENT TO GLAZE ONE 18 CM/7 INCH FRUIT FLAN OR 12-16 TARTLETS

MICROWAVE TIP Mix the arrowroot with a little of the syrup in a medium bowl. Add the remaining syrup and cook on High for 1 minute. Stir, then cook for 1 minute more or until the glaze clears. Add food colouring and lemon juice as above.

ALMOND PASTE AND MARZIPAN

Either almond paste or marzipan may be used to cover a Battenburg cake, to fill a simnel cake or as a base for royal icing on a Christmas or wedding cake. Both almond paste and marzipan provide a flat, even surface over which icing will flow in a smooth glossy sheet, and as a bonus, will prevent crumbs from the cake spoiling the appearance of the icing. Marzipan resembles almond paste, but is smoother and more malleable. It is easier to use than almond paste when making moulded decorations or petits fours. For use and quantities required for individual cakes see opposite.

MARZIPAN

1 egg
1 egg white
200 g/7 oz icing sugar, sifted
200 g/7 oz ground almonds
5 ml/1 tsp lemon juice
few drops of almond essence

Whisk the egg, egg white and icing sugar in a heatproof bowl over hot water until thick and creamy. Add the ground almonds with the lemon juice and almond essence and mix well. Work in more lemon juice, if necessary. When cool enough to handle, knead lightly until smooth. Use as for almond paste, or for making moulded decorations (see page 94).

MAKES ABOUT 400 G/14 OZ

ALMOND PASTE

This recipe makes a pale, creamy yellow coloured paste that can be used to cover and decorate cakes, as well as for a base coat before applying icing.

225 g/8 oz ground almonds
100 g/4 oz caster sugar
100 g/4 oz icing sugar
5 ml/1 tsp lemon juice
few drops of almond essence
1 egg, beaten

Using a coarse sieve, sift the almonds, caster sugar and icing sugar into a mixing bowl. Add the lemon juice, almond essence and sufficient egg to bind the ingredients together. Knead lightly with the fingertips until smooth.

Wrap in cling film and overwrap in foil or a plastic bag to prevent the paste drying out. Store in a cool place until required.

MAKES ABOUT 450 G/1 LB

> **MRS BEETON'S TIP** Don't knead the paste too much: this can draw the oils from the almonds and make the paste greasy. It will then be unsuitable as a base for icing.

COOKED ALMOND PASTE

This makes a smoother and more malleable paste than the uncooked mixture. Use it for moulding decorations and for covering wedding cakes.

450 g/1 lb granulated sugar
1.25 ml/¼ tsp cream of tartar
300 g/11 oz ground almonds
2 egg whites
5 ml/1 tsp almond essence
50 g/2 oz icing sugar

Place the sugar with 150 ml/¼ pint water in a saucepan over moderate heat. Stir occasionally until all the sugar has melted, then bring the syrup to the boil.

In a cup, dissolve the cream of tartar in 5 ml/1 tsp water and stir it into the syrup. Boil, without stirring, until the syrup registers 115°C/240°F on a sugar thermometer, the soft ball stage (see Mrs Beeton's Tip).

Remove the pan from the heat and immediately stir in the ground almonds followed by the unbeaten egg whites and almond essence. Return the pan to a low heat and cook, stirring constantly, for 2 minutes. Set the pan aside until the mixture is cool enough to handle.

Sift the icing sugar on to a clean work surface, place the marzipan in the centre and knead with the fingertips until the sugar is absorbed. If the marzipan is sticky, leave to cool for longer and then add a little more icing sugar, if necessary. Cover lightly until cold, then wrap and store in a cool place, as for almond paste.

MAKES 900 G/2 LB

> **MRS BEETON'S TIP** If you do not have a sugar thermometer, drop about 2.5 ml/½ tsp syrup into a bowl of iced water. If you can mould the syrup between your fingers to make a soft ball, the syrup is ready.

ALMOND PASTE/MARZIPAN

Quick guide to quantities required to cover fruit cakes

Round	Quantity	Square	Quantity
15 cm/6 inches	350 g/12 oz	15 cm/6 inches	500 g/18 oz
18 cm/7 inches	500 g/18 oz	18 cm/7 inches	575 g/1¼ lb
20 cm/8 inches	575 g/1¼ lb	20 cm/8 inches	800 g/1¾ lb
23 cm/9 inches	800 g/1¾ lb	23 cm/9 inches	900 g/2 lb
25 cm/10 inches	900 g/2 lb	25 cm/10 inches	1 kg/2¼ lb
28 cm/11 inches	1 kg/2¼ lb	28 cm/11 inches	1.1 kg/2½ lb
30 cm/12 inches	1.25 kg/2½ lb	30 cm/12 inches	1.4 kg/3 lb

BUTTER ICINGS AND FUDGE ICINGS

These are soft icings made with butter and icing sugar which may be used for filling or covering lighter cakes and gâteaux. On drying, an outer crust forms but the icing remains soft underneath. The iced cake should be stored away from heat or direct sunlight.

Use unsalted butter if possible and flavour the icing as required. Soften the butter before using or try using a butter mixture that spreads easily even when chilled – these usually contain vegetable oil and therefore little or no extra liquid will be required when mixing the icing.

When adding food colouring to butter-based icings, do not expect clear colours. Avoid adding blue, as the yellow in the butter will turn it green!

All these icings may be spread with a palette knife or piped using a savoy nozzle.

★ **FREEZER TIP** Buttercream can be frozen successfully, unless the recipe contains egg, in which case it may curdle. When piping with buttercream it is necessary to make slightly more than required; however any leftovers can be frozen for future use as a filling for cakes. The prepared buttercream can be flavoured before or after freezing. Pack the buttercream in a rigid container, then leave it to thaw in the refrigerator or in a cool place and beat it thoroughly before use.

RICH BUTTERCREAM

This buttercream is enriched by the addition of an egg yolk. Use only very fresh eggs and make sure that all utensils used to prepare the buttercream are perfectly clean.

1 egg yolk
200 g/7 oz icing sugar, sifted
100 g/4 oz butter, softened
flavouring

Beat the egg yolk in a mixing bowl, adding the sugar gradually until the mixture is smooth. Beat in the butter, a little at a time with the flavouring.

SUFFICIENT TO FILL AND TOP A 20 CM/8 INCH CAKE

BUTTERCREAM

100 g/4 oz butter, softened
15 ml/1 tbsp milk or fruit juice
225 g/8 oz icing sugar, sifted

In a mixing bowl, cream the butter with the milk or juice and gradually work in the icing sugar. Beat the icing until light and fluffy. Alternatively, work all the ingredients in a food processor, removing the plunger for the final mixing to allow air to enter the buttercream mixture.

SUFFICIENT TO FILL AND TOP A 20 CM/8 INCH CAKE

FLUFFY BUTTERCREAM

2 egg whites
200 g/7 oz icing sugar, sifted
100 g/4 oz butter, softened
flavouring

Whisk the egg whites in a large bowl until stiff. Add the icing sugar, a third at a time, whisking between each addition until the mixture forms peaks.

In a mixing bowl, cream the butter until light and fluffy. Gradually fold in the meringue mixture. Flavour as required.

SUFFICIENT TO FILL AND TOP A 20 CM/8 INCH CAKE

VARIATIONS

These flavourings may be used with any of the buttercreams.

CHOCOLATE BUTTERCREAM Grate 50 g/2 oz block plain chocolate. Place it in a basin over hot water with 15 ml/1 tbsp milk, stir until dissolved, then cool. Use instead of the liquid in the plain buttercream.
COFFEE BUTTERCREAM Dissolve 5 ml/1 tsp instant coffee in 15 ml/1 tbsp hot water. Cool before use. Use instead of the milk or fruit juice in the plain buttercream.
LEMON OR ORANGE BUTTERCREAM Use 15 ml/1 tbsp juice and a little grated rind.
VANILLA BUTTERCREAM Add 2.5 ml/½ tsp vanilla essence with the milk.
WALNUT BUTTERCREAM Add 25 g/1 oz chopped walnuts.

FRENCH BUTTER ICING

This resembles a frosting, in that the sugar is boiled and added as a syrup to the other ingredients. The high percentage of butter, however, assures it of a place in this section.

50 g/2 oz granulated sugar
1 egg yolk
150 g/5 oz butter, cut into small pieces

Mix the sugar with 125 ml/4 fl oz water in a small heavy saucepan. Stirring occasionally, heat gently until all the sugar has dissolved. Increase the heat and boil, without stirring, until the syrup registers 105°C/220°F on a sugar thermometer, the thread stage (see Mrs Beeton's Tip).

Place the egg yolk in a bowl, whisk lightly, then gradually whisk in the syrup. Continue whisking until cool, then add the butter, a little at a time, whisking constantly.

SUFFICIENT TO COAT THE TOP AND SIDES OF A 20 CM/8 INCH CAKE

VARIATION

CHOCOLATE FRENCH BUTTER ICING Break up 100 g/4 oz plain dark chocolate and stir into the warm syrup mixture until melted. Beat until smooth and glossy.

MRS BEETON'S TIP If you do not have a sugar thermometer, test the syrup by dipping a spoon in the syrup and then pressing another spoon on to the back of it and pulling away. If a thread forms, the syrup is ready.

CHOCOLATE FUDGE ICING

100 g/4 oz plain chocolate, broken into
  pieces
50 g/2 oz butter, cut up
1 egg, beaten
175 g/6 oz icing sugar, sifted

Combine the chocolate and butter in a
heatproof bowl. Set over hot water until the
chocolate has melted. Beat in the egg, then
remove the bowl from the heat and stir in
half the icing sugar. Beat in the remaining
sugar and continue beating until the icing is
smooth and cold. Use immediately.

**SUFFICIENT TO FILL AND TOP A 20 CM/8
INCH CAKE**

VARIATIONS

**CHOCOLATE WALNUT FUDGE
ICING** Add 50 g/2 oz of finely chopped
walnuts to the icing just before spreading it
on the cake.
   CHOCOLATE RUM FUDGE ICING
Add 30 ml/2 tbsp of rum to the icing with the
egg and continue as in the main recipe.
   **CHOCOLATE ORANGE FUDGE
ICING** Add the grated rind of 1 orange to
the chocolate and butter. Continue as in the
main recipe.

☀ **MICROWAVE TIP** Melt the
chocolate with the butter in a small
bowl on Medium for 1-2 minutes.

DARK FUDGE ICING

75 g/3 oz butter
75 g/3 oz soft dark brown sugar
30 ml/2 tbsp milk
225 g/8 oz icing sugar, sifted

Combine the butter, brown sugar and
milk in a saucepan. Place over moderate
heat, stirring occasionally until the sugar has
melted. Remove the pan from the heat, add
the icing sugar and beat until cool. Use
immediately.

**SUFFICIENT TO COAT THE TOP AND
SIDES OF A 20 CM/8 INCH CAKE**

VARIATIONS

DARK HONEY FUDGE ICING Use 15
ml/1 tbsp of honey instead of 25 g/1 oz of the
sugar in the main recipe.
   COFFEE FUDGE ICING Add 5 ml/1
tsp of instant coffee to the butter, sugar and
milk mixture. Continue as in the recipe.
   DARK NUT FUDGE ICING Stir in 30
ml/2 tbsp of smooth peanut butter before
adding the icing sugar. This icing can be used
to sandwich plain biscuits in pairs or it can be
used as a topping for chocolate brownies or
small plain cakes.
   DARK GINGER FUDGE ICING Add a
pinch of ground ginger to the butter, sugar
and milk mixture. Beat in 30 ml/2 tbsp of
finely chopped preserved stem ginger or
crystallised ginger. This icing makes an
unusual topping for gingerbread.

☀ **MICROWAVE TIP** Melt the butter
and sugar in a bowl with the milk on
Medium for 1-2 minutes.

GLACÉ ICING

Glacé icing is mainly used as a covering for small cakes, sponge cakes or other light cakes. It is quick and easy to make and therefore ideal for simple, informal cakes. It gives a smooth, slightly crisp coating that complements piped buttercream edges. This icing can also be used to coat plain biscuits. Basically a mixture of icing sugar and warm water, it may also contain flavourings and colourings or extra ingredients as in the Chocolate Glacé Icing on page 28.

There is also a recipe for a Glacé Fondant (overleaf) which is based on the same ingredients as glacé icing but it is heated and enriched with a little butter to give a very glossy result. It should not be confused with Traditional Fondant which is a more formal icing.

The consistency of the icing is all important; it should be stiff enough to coat the back of a wooden spoon thickly, otherwise it will run off the surface of the cake and drip down the sides.

Glacé icing should be used immediately. If left to stand, even for a short while, the surface should be covered completely with damp greaseproof paper or cling film. Any crystallised icing on the surface should be scraped off before use. Because the icing sets so quickly, any additional decorations must be put on as soon as the cake is iced, or the surface will crack

The choice of decorations to use with glacé icing is important. Do not use decorations liable to melt, run or be damaged by damp. Crystallised flower petals, chocolate decorations and small sweets which will shed colour should not be used.

GLACÉ ICING

This simple, basic icing is quickly prepared and is ideal for topping a plain sponge cake or a batch of small cakes. Make the icing just before it is to be used and keep any extra decorations to the minimum.

100 g/4 oz icing sugar, sifted
food colouring, optional

Place the icing sugar in a bowl. Using a wooden spoon gradually stir in sufficient warm water (about 15 ml/1 tbsp) to create icing whose consistency will thickly coat the back of the spoon. Take care not to add too much liquid or the icing will be too runny. At first the icing will seem quite stiff, but it slackens rapidly as the icing sugar absorbs the water. Stir in 1-2 drops of food colouring, if required.

SUFFICIENT TO COVER THE TOP OF ONE 18 CM/7 INCH CAKE

VARIATIONS

LEMON OR ORANGE GLACÉ ICING Use 15 ml/1 tbsp strained lemon or orange juice instead of the water.

COFFEE GLACÉ ICING Dissolve 5 ml/1 tsp instant coffee in 15 ml/1 tbsp warm water and add instead of the water in the main recipe.

LIQUEUR-FLAVOURED GLACÉ ICING Replace half the water with the liqueur of your choice.

CHOCOLATE GLACÉ ICING

An icing that contains dessert chocolate and/or butter will thicken and set more readily than one which merely contains a liquid.

50 g/2 oz plain chocolate, broken into
    small pieces
knob of butter
100 g/4 oz icing sugar, sifted

Combine the chocolate and butter in a heatproof bowl. Add 15 ml/1 tbsp water. Place the bowl over hot water. When the chocolate has melted, stir the mixture, gradually adding the sugar. Add a little more water, if necessary, to give a smooth coating consistency. Use at once.

SUFFICIENT TO COAT THE TOP OF ONE 18 CM/7 INCH CAKE

☀ **MICROWAVE TIP** Melt the chocolate, butter and water in a bowl on Medium for 1-2 minutes.

GLACÉ FONDANT

225 g/8 oz icing sugar, sifted
2.5 ml/½ tsp lemon juice
knob of butter

Combine the icing sugar and lemon juice in a small saucepan and mix well. Add the butter and cook over a low heat, stirring with a wooden spoon, until the butter has melted and the icing is well blended. Immediately pour over the cake.

SUFFICIENT TO COVER THE TOP OF A 20 CM/8 INCH CAKE

FROSTINGS

Frosting is usually spread thickly all over a cake, covering the sides as well as the top. When set, it is crisper than glacé icing, because the sugar is heated or boiled when making it. It should have a soft, spreading consistency when applied. Have the cake ready before starting to make the frosting.

AMERICAN FROSTING

225 g/8 oz granulated sugar
pinch of cream of tartar
1 egg white
2.5 ml/½ tsp vanilla essence or a few drops
    lemon juice

Combine the sugar and cream of tartar in a small saucepan. Add 60 ml/4 tbsp water. Place over a low heat, stirring occasionally until the sugar has melted. Heat, without stirring until the syrup registers 115°C/240°F, the soft ball stage, on a sugar thermometer (see Mrs Beeton's Tip, page 23). Remove from the heat.

In a large grease-free bowl, whisk the egg white until stiff. Pour on the syrup in a thin stream, whisking continuously. Add the flavouring and continue to whisk until the frosting is thick and glossy and stands in peaks when the whisk is lifted.

Quickly spread over the cake. As the frosting cools, it may be swirled with a knife and lifted to form peaks.

SUFFICIENT TO COVER THE TOP AND SIDES OF ONE 18 CM/7 INCH CAKE

🥣 **MRS BEETON'S TIP** Make sure that both bowl and whisk are free from grease, otherwise the frosting will not whisk up well.

QUICK AMERICAN FROSTING

175 g/6 oz caster sugar
1 egg white
pinch of cream of tartar
pinch of salt

Heat a mixing bowl over a large saucepan of simmering water. Remove the bowl and place all the ingredients in it. Add 30 ml/2 tbsp water and whisk with a rotary or electric whisk until the ingredients are well mixed.

Remove the saucepan of simmering water from the heat, place the bowl over the water, and whisk until the frosting forms soft peaks. Use immediately.

SUFFICIENT TO COVER THE TOP AND SIDES OF ONE 18 CM/7 INCH CAKE

CARAMEL FROSTING

350 g/12 oz soft light brown sugar
1.25 ml/¼ tsp cream of tartar
2 egg whites
pinch of salt
5 ml/1 tsp vanilla essence

Heat a mixing bowl over a large saucepan of boiling water. Remove the bowl and add all the ingredients except the vanilla essence. Add 150 ml/¼ pint water and whisk with a rotary or electric whisk until well mixed.

Place the bowl over the water and continue to whisk until the frosting forms soft peaks. Remove the bowl from the water, add the essence and whisk the frosting for about 2 minutes more, until it reaches a spreading consistency. Use immediately.

SUFFICIENT TO FILL, TOP AND COVER THE SIDES OF ONE 18 CM/7 INCH CAKE

WHIPPED CREAM FROSTING

The addition of gelatine not only makes the cream more stable but also increases the volume.

10 ml/2 tsp gelatine
rind and juice of ½ lemon
pinch of salt
30 ml/2 tbsp icing sugar
250 ml/8 fl oz double cream

Place 30 ml/2 tbsp tepid water in a bowl and sprinkle the gelatine into the water. Stand the bowl over a saucepan of hot water and stir until the gelatine has dissolved completely.

Combine the lemon rind and juice, salt and icing sugar in a blender. Add 30 ml/2 tbsp of the cream, with the gelatine mixture. Process for 1 minute. Alternatively, whisk hard for 3 minutes.

Pour the mixture into a bowl and chill until it has the consistency of unbeaten egg white.

Whip the remaining cream until it forms soft peaks and fold it carefully into the gelatine mixture. Chill.

SUFFICIENT TO FILL AND TOP ONE 20 CM/ 8 INCH CAKE

TRADITIONAL FONDANT

Not to be confused with moulding icings or sugar paste icing. Traditional fondant is poured over the cake. It sets to a dry, shiny finish that remains soft inside. It is widely used by commercial confectioners for petits fours. Some specialist shops sell fondant icing in powdered form. This is a boon because small quantities may be made up by adding water or stock syrup. To make up and use fondant icing see page 72. You will need a sugar thermometer to make fondant.

450 g/1 lb caster or lump sugar
20 ml/4 tsp liquid glucose

Put the sugar in a heavy-bottomed saucepan which is absolutely free from grease. Add 150 ml/¼ pint water and heat gently until the sugar has completely dissolved. Stir very occasionally and use a wet pastry brush to wipe away any crystals that form on the sides of the pan. When the sugar has dissolved add the liquid glucose and boil to 115°C/240°F, the soft ball stage (see Mrs Beeton's Tip, page 23), without stirring. Keep the sides of the pan clean by brushing with the wet brush when necessary. Remove from the heat and allow the bubbles in the mixture to subside.

Pour the mixture slowly into the middle of a wetted marble slab and allow to cool a little. Work the sides to the middle with a sugar scraper or palette knife to make a smaller mass.

With a wooden spatula in one hand and the scraper in the other, make a figure of eight with the spatula, keeping the mixture together with the scraper. Work until the mass is completely white.

Break off small amounts and knead well, then knead all the small pieces together to form a ball.

Store in a screw-topped jar, or wrap closely in several layers of polythene. When required, dilute with stock syrup (below).

MAKES ABOUT 450 G/1 LB FONDANT

🍲 **MRS BEETON'S TIP** To give the fondant a hint of flavour use vanilla sugar instead of ordinary caster sugar or lump sugar. Vanilla sugar is made by placing a vanilla pod in a jar of caster sugar. The sugar should be left for a few weeks, shaking the jar occasionally, until it has absorbed the flavour of the vanilla.

STOCK SYRUP

Use this syrup when diluting fondant. It may also be kneaded into commercially made almond paste to make the paste more pliable.

150 g/5 oz granulated sugar

Put the sugar in a saucepan and add 150 ml/¼ pint water. Heat, stirring occasionally, until the sugar has dissolved, then boil without stirring for 3 minutes. Use a spoon to remove any scum that rises to the surface.

Allow the syrup to cool, then strain into a jar and cover with a lid. If not required immediately, store in a cool place (not the refrigerator) for up to 2 months.

QUICK FONDANT

30 ml/2 tbsp liquid glucose
225 g/8 oz icing sugar, sifted
food colouring (optional)

Mix the liquid glucose with 30 ml/2 tbsp boiling water in a large bowl. Beat in the icing sugar gradually, adding a few drops of food colouring, if desired.

Place the bowl over a pan of hot water to warm the icing before using for coating. Add a few drops of water if the icing becomes too thick.

SUFFICIENT TO COVER THE TOP AND SIDES OF ONE 18 CM/7 INCH CAKE

MICROWAVE TIP Put the glucose in a bowl with 60 ml/4 tbsp cold water. Heat on Medium for 30 seconds and add the icing sugar and food colouring as above.

SYRUP-BASED FONDANT

45 ml/3 tbsp warm Sugar Syrup (recipe follows)
275 g/10 oz icing sugar, sifted
food colouring, optional

Place the sugar syrup in a bowl and beat in sufficient icing sugar to coat the back of the spoon. Add a few drops of food colouring, if desired. Use at once or allow to cool, knead well and store as for fondant.

SUFFICIENT TO COVER THE TOP AND SIDES OF ONE 23 CM/9 INCH CAKE

SUGAR SYRUP

An essential part of Syrup-based Fondant icing, this may also be added to chocolate when piping. Flavoured with liqueur or fruit juices it is ideal for moistening cakes. It will keep for up to two months without refrigeration.

225 g/8 oz granulated sugar
1.25 ml/¼ tsp cream of tartar

Place the sugar with 15 ml/1 tbsp water in a small, heavy-bottomed saucepan over low heat and stir occasionally until the sugar has melted. Increase the heat and bring to the boil.

In a cup, dissolve the cream of tartar in 5 ml/1 tsp water, add to the saucepan and continue to boil the syrup, without stirring, until it registers 105°C/220°F on a sugar thermometer, the thread stage (see Mrs Beeton's Tip, page 25).

Remove the syrup from the heat, cool, strain and store in a screw-topped jar.

MAKES 125 ML/4 FL OZ

MRS BEETON'S TIP Always heat a sugar thermometer in hot water before putting it into the boiling syrup. To register the correct temperature, the thermometer must not touch the base of the pan. After use rest the thermometer on a saucer until it is cool enough to be washed in hot soapy water.

ROYAL ICING

Royal Icing is used for special celebration cakes, especially for wedding cakes, because the icing has sufficient strength when it sets hard to hold the tiers. The icing cannot be applied directly to the cake because it would drag the crumbs and discolour badly, so rich fruit cakes are usually covered with a layer of almond paste or marzipan before the royal icing is applied.

Traditionalists believe that royal icing can only be made successfully with egg whites and hard beating, but dried egg white or albumen powder is fast gaining in popularity because the icing can be made in a food mixer or with an electric whisk. Whichever method you choose, the secret of successful royal icing work, be it flat icing or piping, depends upon making the icing to the correct consistency. This is discussed further on the opposite page.

ROYAL ICING

Quick guide to quantities of Royal Icing required to cover cakes (sufficient for 3 coats)

ROUND	ROYAL ICING
15 cm/6 inch	575 g/1¼ lb
18 cm/7 inch	675 g/1½ lb
20 cm/8 inch	800 g/1¾ lb
23 cm/9 inch	900 g/2 lb
25 cm/10 inch	1 kg/2¼ lb
28 cm/11 inch	1.25 kg/2¾ lb
30 cm/12 inch	1.4 kg/3 lb

SQUARE	ROYAL ICING
15 cm/6 inch	675 g/1½ lb
18 cm/7 inch	800 g/1¾ lb
20 cm/8 inch	900 g/2 lb
23 cm/9 inch	1 kg/2¼ lb
25 cm/10 inch	1.25 kg/2¾ lb
28 cm/11 inch	1.4 kg/3 lb
30 cm/12 inch	1.5 kg/3¼ lb

ROYAL ICING (USING EGG WHITE)

It is vital to ensure that the bowl is clean and free from grease. Use a wooden spoon kept solely for the purpose and do not be tempted to skimp on the beating – insufficient beating will produce an off-white icing with a heavy, sticky texture.

2 egg whites
450 g/1 lb icing sugar, sifted

Place the egg whites in a bowl and break them up with a fork. Gradually beat in about two-thirds of the icing sugar with a wooden spoon, and continue beating for about 15 minutes until the icing is pure white and forms soft peaks. Add the remaining icing sugar, if necessary, to attain this texture. Cover the bowl with cling film and place a dampened tea towel on top. Place the bowl inside a plastic bag if storing overnight or for longer.

Before use, lightly beat the icing to burst any air bubbles that have risen to the surface. Adjust the consistency for flat icing or piping.

SUFFICIENT TO COAT THE TOP AND SIDES OF A 20 CM/8 INCH CAKE

MRS BEETON'S TIP If the icing is to be used for a single cake, glycerine may be added to prevent it from becoming too brittle when dry. Add 2.5 ml/½ tsp glycerine during the final beating. Do not, however, use glycerine for a tiered cake where the icing must be hard in order to hold the tiers.

Three-tiered Wedding Cake (page 127)

Single-tier Wedding Cake (page 128)

Girl's Christening Cake (page 129)

Boy's Christening Cake (page 130)

Twenty-first Birthday Cake (page 131)

Musical Notes Birthday Cake (page 132)

Brush Embroidery Cakes (page 132)

Father Christmas Cake (page 134)

ROYAL ICING (USING DRIED EGG WHITE)

15 ml/1 tbsp dried egg white (albumen powder)
450 g/1 lb icing sugar

Place 60 ml/4 tbsp warm water in a bowl. Add the dried egg white, mix thoroughly and leave for 10-15 minutes. Whisk with a fork and strain the mixture into a mixing bowl.

Gradually beat in about two-thirds of the icing sugar and continue beating for 5 minutes in a food mixer or with a hand-held electric whisk until the icing is pure white, light and stands in soft peaks. Add extra icing sugar, if necessary.

Cover and use as for the royal icing (using egg white) except that fewer air bubbles will be present.

VARIATION

ALBUMEN SUBSTITUTE May be used in place of albumen powder. Sift it into the bowl. Beat for 5 minutes as above.

 MRS BEETON'S TIP Be careful not to beat the icing for too long or it may break when piped.

QUICK GUIDE TO CONSISTENCY OF ROYAL ICING FOR DIFFERENT APPLICATIONS

Once the required consistency has been achieved, cover the icing with a damp cloth, even during use.

CONSISTENCY	DESCRIPTION	USE
Thin Icing	Just finds its own level when gently tapped	Run-outs and flooding
Soft Peak (1)	Forms a soft peak when the spoon is lifted out but readily falls over	Embroidery work. Very fine 00 writing nozzles
Soft Peak (2)	Forms a soft peak but only tip bends over	Flat icing
Medium Peak	Firmer peak that holds its shape	Most piping except patterns using the larger nozzles
Firm Peak	Stiffer peak but still soft enough to push through a nozzle without excessive pressure	Petals for flowers, large shell and similar nozzles

MOULDING ICINGS

SUGAR PASTE

Since the introduction of this versatile and easy-to-use icing from the humid regions of Australia and South Africa, where royal icing does not dry at all well, cake decorating has been quite revolutionised. Sugar paste, also known as decorating icing or mallow paste, resembles commercially made marzipan in its properties, texture and application (although not in colour or flavour). Sometimes it is referred to as fondant icing but it must not be confused with a traditional, pouring fondant. It is rolled out and moulded over the cake. In many cases this makes a base layer of marzipan unnecessary. It is, therefore, widely used on sponge cakes and because it can be easily coloured, makes wonderful novelty cakes.

There are several recipes for sugar paste: try them all and find the one which suits you best.

If well wrapped in polythene the icing will keep for several weeks in a cupboard. Do not store it in the refrigerator as it would lose its elasticity and become difficult to work.

Sugar paste is malleable and may be moulded into shapes and petals for flowers. When worked into very thin pieces, it will dry hard and brittle and can be used for plaques and Garrett frills. For more information, see Moulded Decorations (page 94).

As a general rule, it is best not to freeze a whole cake covered in this icing, especially if different colours have been used. This is because the icing becomes wet and the colours may run into each other. If only a small area of the cake has paste icing, as in a novelty cake covered in buttercream with moulded icing features, the cake can be frozen. When required, it must be taken out of the freezer, all wrappings removed and left at room temperature for 4-5 hours to allow the icing to dry off.

SUGAR PASTE

Quick guide to quantities required to cover cakes

ROUND	SUGAR PASTE
15 cm/6 inch	450 g/1 lb
18 cm/7 inch	575 g/1¼ lb
20 cm/8 inch	675 g/1½ lb
23 cm/9 inch	800 g/1¾ lb
25 cm/10 inch	900 g/2 lb
28 cm/11 inch	1 kg/2¼ lb
30 cm/12 inch	1.1 kg/2½ lb

SQUARE	SUGAR PASTE
15 cm/6 inch	575 g/1¼ lb
18 cm/7 inch	675 g/1½ lb
20 cm/8 inch	800 g/1¾ lb
23 cm/9 inch	900 g/2 lb
25 cm/10 inch	1 kg/2¼ lb
28 cm/11 inch	1.1 kg/2½ lb
30 cm/12 inch	1.4 kg/3 lb

SUGAR PASTE

675 g/1½ lb icing sugar, sifted
2 medium egg whites
30 ml/2 tbsp warmed liquid glucose
5 ml/1 tsp glycerine

Place the icing sugar in a clean, greasefree bowl. Add the remaining ingredients and work together with either a clean wooden spoon or the fingertips. Place the rough mixture on a clean surface dusted with icing sugar and knead hard for several minutes until smooth, pliable and not sticky, adding a little extra icing sugar if necessary. Wrap the sugar paste in polythene and leave to rest for 24 hours before using.

SUFFICIENT TO COVER THE TOP AND SIDES OF A 20 CM/8 INCH CAKE

GELATINE-BASED SUGAR PASTE

The gelatine replaces the egg white in this recipe and helps to keep the icing malleable. Be careful to measure the ingredients accurately. This paste is ideal for covering cakes and for making cut-out decorations, but it is not firm enough for making moulded decorations.

10 ml/2 tsp gelatine
5 ml/1 tsp glycerine
15 ml/1 tbsp warmed liquid glucose
about 450 g/1 lb icing sugar, sifted

Dissolve the gelatine in 20 ml/4 tsp warm water (see Mrs Beeton's Tip). Add the glycerine and liquid glucose.

Place the icing sugar in a large bowl, pour over the gelatine mixture and work the mixture together with a clean wooden spoon or the fingertips, adding a little extra icing sugar if necessary, Knead the paste until smooth. Use warm or wrap well and store.

SUFFICIENT TO COVER THE TOP AND SIDES OF A 15 CM/6 INCH CAKE

MRS BEETON'S TIP To dissolve the gelatine, sprinkle the powder over the warm water in a small bowl. Stand the bowl over a saucepan of hot water and stir until the gelatine has dissolved completely.

MICROWAVE TIP For easy measuring, the liquid glucose may be softened for a few seconds on Defrost. Be careful not to make it too hot.

MOULDING PASTE

This icing can be readily made from storecupboard ingredients but it is not as malleable as the sugar pastes and needs to be worked more quickly. The colour of the fat determines the colour of the finished paste.

25 g/1 oz butter
15 ml/1 tbsp lemon juice
350 g/12 oz icing sugar, sifted

Combine the butter and lemon juice in a small saucepan with 15 ml/1 tbsp water. Place over a low heat until the butter has melted.

Add 100 g/4 oz of the icing sugar, mix well and stir for 2 minutes or until the mixture begins to boil. Do not overcook. Immediately remove the pan from the heat and stir in 100 g/4 oz of the remaining icing sugar. Place the mixture in a clean bowl and beat with a wooden spoon, gradually adding extra icing sugar until it forms a soft dough.

Place the dough on a clean surface lightly dusted with icing sugar and knead until smooth and cool. Use immediately or cover until cold, then wrap in polythene.

SUFFICIENT TO COVER THE TOP OF A 20 CM/8 INCH CAKE

VARIATION

WHITE MOULDING PASTE Use a white fat but add a few extra drops of lemon juice, or rose water or almond essence to flavour.

MRS BEETON'S TIP If the paste becomes too dry to handle when stored, sprinkle with a little cooled, boiled water and re-seal bag. Leave for several hours to soften.

FILLINGS

If an icing or frosting makes an immediate impact, a filling is a taste of the unexpected. A good filling should complement a cake or gâteau, either enhancing an existing flavour or providing an interesting contrast without being overwhelming. This section of the book introduces lots of new ideas alongside old favourites like jam, lemon curd, fresh cream and fruit purées. When using fruit, make sure that the filling is not too wet, or the cake will become soggy.

Most of the buttercreams listed in an earlier section may be used as fillings, and more recipes will be found in the sections on Healthier Alternatives and Custards.

Use the fillings for large and small cakes, tray bakes and gâteaux. Multi-layered, and filled and topped with soft icing or cream, a gâteau is usually eaten with a fork or spoon, often as a dessert. A cake generally has a firmer filling, and may be held in the hand to be eaten.

RUM AND WALNUT FILLING

Use this as a filling for spice cakes or light fruity cakes.

50 g/2 oz butter
75 g/3 oz soft light brown sugar
15 ml/1 tbsp rum
50 g/2 oz walnuts, chopped

Cream the butter and sugar together in a mixing bowl until soft. Gradually add the rum and beat well until the icing is light and fluffy. Fold in the walnuts.

SUFFICIENT FOR A SINGLE LAYER IN ONE 18 CM/7 INCH CAKE

COCONUT FILLING

This crunchy filling is suitable for sponges or for slightly heavier cakes similar to Madeira cakes. It can also be used as an unusual topping for small cakes.

50 g/2 oz icing sugar, sifted
1 egg yolk
15 ml/1 tbsp lemon juice
25 g/1 oz desiccated coconut

Place the icing sugar, egg yolk and lemon juice in a small bowl and mix to a smooth paste. Place the bowl over a saucepan of hot water over a low heat and cook the mixture for 5-7 minutes, stirring constantly, until the mixture thickly coats the back of the wooden spoon. Remove the bowl from the heat and stir in the coconut. Leave to cool and thicken before use.

SUFFICIENT FOR A SINGLE LAYER IN ONE 18 CM/7 INCH CAKE

VARIATION

Toast the desiccated coconut under a grill or replace with ground toasted nuts.

MRS BEETON'S TIP These full-flavoured, nutty fillings go very well with cakes that are slightly more dense in texture or those that are well flavoured, for example chocolate cakes. Lighter fillings with a smooth texture are more suitable for airy, fatless sponge cakes.

CREAM FILLINGS

Fresh cream is still a prime favourite as a filling for gâteaux and afternoon tea cakes. Double cream has the best flavour and may be whipped and piped in much the same way as royal icing. Once whipped, it may be frozen on the decorated gâteaux and will not lose its shape when thawed. To reduce the risk of over-whipping, which might cause the cream to separate in hot weather, add 15 ml/ 1 tbsp milk to each 150 ml/¼ pint cream or replace up to one-third of the double cream with single cream. There is no need to add sugar to whipped cream.

TO WHIP THE CREAM

Choose a cool area of the kitchen in which to work and chill the bowl and whisk before use, by placing them in the refrigerator or freezer for a few minutes. A small wire balloon whisk is the best utensil, but for large quantities a hand-held electric whisk may be used with care.

Stand the bowl on a wet cloth or a non-slip surface, add the cream and tip the bowl. While whipping, incorporate as much air as possible. If using an electric whisk, start on high and reduce speed to low as the cream begins to thicken. Be very careful not to overwhip. Stop whipping as soon as the cream will stand in soft peaks and has doubled in volume.

The cream will continue to thicken slightly on standing and when piped, so stop whipping just before you think the cream is ready. It should be smooth and shiny in appearance. Overwhipped cream will 'frill' at the edges when piped.

For best results, use the whipped cream immediately, or cover and store in the refrigerator until required, giving it a gentle stir before use.

If the finished gâteau is to stand in a warm room for any length of time, whip in 5 ml/1 tsp gelatine, dissolved in 10 ml/2 tsp warm water and cooled. See also Whipped Cream Frosting (page 29).

FLAVOURINGS

Add any flavouring to cream when it has been whipped to soft peaks. Lemon or orange juice, liqueur or sherry may be used and should be added gradually during the final whipping. Once the cream has been whipped, finely chopped nuts, glacé fruits or grated citrus rind may be added.

REDUCING THE FAT CONTENT

For a low-fat whipped cream, replace up to one third with low or full-fat plain yogurt. This will not only make the cream less rich, but will prevent overwhipping and keep the cream smooth and shiny.

FREEZING

Cakes decorated with cream should be frozen and stored in a large domed plastic box. Alternatively, open freeze and then cocoon carefully in a dome of foil. Label well to avoid other items being inadvertently placed on top.

To thaw, remove the wrappings and thaw the cakes in a cool place, refrigerator or microwave (following the manufacturer's directions).

Small quantities of leftover cream may be whipped with a little caster sugar and piped in small stars on non-stick baking parchment for freezing. They may then be lifted off and placed, still frozen, on desserts and gâteaux for instant decoration.

CUSTARD FILLINGS

Confectioners' Custard, sometimes called Crème Patissière, makes an excellent filling for cakes. Thickened with eggs, flour or cornflour the custard sets to a thick cream when cold. Mock Cream is a simple filling based on milk thickened with cornflour and enriched with butter, while Quick Diplomat Cream is richer still, with double cream used as its base.

Unless using a double saucepan, it is easier to make these custards with yolks rather than whole eggs as the whites cook more quickly and lumps of cooked egg white may spoil the texture.

Vanilla sugar may be used instead of caster sugar in the recipes that follow. The vanilla pod or essence should then be omitted.

To prevent the formation of a skin on the cooked custard, press a dampened piece of greaseproof paper lightly on the surface. Do not use plasticised cling film for this purpose when the custard is hot.

MRS BEETON'S TIP These light fillings, thickened with eggs, go very well with light sponge cakes and gâteaux that are filled or decorated with fresh fruit. They can also be used to decorate cheesecakes. This type of filling should not be frozen as it tends to curdle.

CONFECTIONERS' CUSTARD

300 ml/½ pint milk
1 vanilla pod or a few drops of vanilla
  essence
2 egg yolks
50 g/2 oz caster sugar
25 g/1 oz plain flour

Place the milk and vanilla pod, if used, in a small saucepan and bring to the boil over low heat. Remove from the heat and leave to one side, adding the vanilla essence, if used.

Whisk the egg yolks with the sugar in a bowl until thick and creamy, then add the flour. Remove the vanilla pod and very gradually add the milk to the egg mixture, beating constantly until all has been incorporated. Pour the mixture back into the saucepan and stir over a low heat for 1-2 minutes to cook the flour. The custard should thickly coat the back of the wooden spoon and be smooth and shiny.

Pour the custard into a clean bowl, cover and leave to cool. Beat well then cover again and chill until required.

MAKES ABOUT 300 ML/½ PINT

VARIATIONS

CHOCOLATE CUSTARD Stir 25 g/1 oz grated chocolate into the custard while still hot.

CRÈME ST HONORE Whisk 2 egg whites with 10 ml/2 tsp of caster sugar until stiff. Fold into cold custard. Use for choux pastry or as an alternative cream for gâteaux.

CRÈME FRANGIPANE Omit the vanilla flavouring. Add 40 g/1½ oz finely chopped butter to final cooking. When cold, fold in 75 g/3 oz crushed almond macaroons or 50 g/2 oz ground almonds and a few drops of almond essence.

CONFECTIONERS' CUSTARD WITH BRANDY

25 g/1 oz cornflour
300 ml/½ pint milk
3 egg yolks
40 g/1½ oz caster sugar
2.5 ml/½ tsp brandy, rum or liqueur

In a bowl mix the cornflour with a little milk, then beat in the egg yolks and sugar. Heat the remaining milk in a saucepan until tepid and pour slowly on to the cornflour mixture, stirring constantly. Pour the mixture back into the saucepan and stir over a low heat, without boiling, until the custard thickens and thickly coats the back of the wooden spoon. Remove from the heat, stir in the brandy, rum or liqueur and pour into a clean bowl. Cover and cool, then beat well. Cover again and chill until required.

MAKES ABOUT 300 ML/½ PINT

MOCK CREAM

10 ml/2 tsp cornflour
150 ml/¼ pint milk
50 g/2 oz butter, softened
50 g/2 oz icing or caster sugar
few drops of vanilla or almond essence

Mix the cornflour with a little milk in a small saucepan. Gradually stir in the remaining milk and cook over a low heat, stirring constantly until the mixture thickens. Cover and leave until tepid.

Cream the butter and sugar together in a bowl until light and fluffy. Gradually add the custard mixture to the butter, beating well between each addition. Beat in the essence, cover and chill.

SUFFICIENT FOR 2 LAYERS IN ONE 18 CM/ 7 INCH CAKE

QUICK DIPLOMAT CREAM

15 ml/1 tbsp custard powder
10 ml/2 tsp caster sugar
150 ml/¼ pint milk
150 ml/¼ pint double cream
few drops of vanilla essence

Mix the custard powder and sugar with a little milk in a small saucepan. Gradually stir in the remaining milk and stir over a low heat for 1 minute until thick. Transfer the mixture to a bowl, cover and leave to cool. Beat well then cover again and chill.

In a clean bowl, whisk the cream with the vanilla essence until thick. Beat the custard until smooth and lightly fold in the cream until well blended. Chill until required.

MAKES ABOUT 300 ML/½ PINT

VARIATIONS

ORANGE OR LEMON Fold in 5 ml/1 tsp finely grated orange or lemon rind.
CHOCOLATE Stir 50 g/2 oz grated chocolate into the hot custard.
LIQUEUR Replace the essence with brandy or liqueur.

TOPPINGS

These simple toppings may be prepared in advance and used to quickly decorate and finish a cake or gâteau. Most toppings can be stored in a screw-topped jar or in a cardboard box for several months. For a comprehensive list of shop-bought toppings and decorations see page 14.

COCONUT

Coconut has an interesting texture and makes a good topping on plain cakes. Choose good-quality desiccated coconut with large strands and use plain or colour as follows: Place about 50 g/2 oz coconut in a screw top jar, leaving at least 2.5 cm/1 inch space at the top. Add a few drops of food colouring (liquid colours are best), screw on the lid and shake the jar vigorously for a few minutes until the coconut is evenly coloured. Use the same day or spread the coconut out on a piece of greaseproof paper and leave in a warm place to dry before storing in a dry screw-topped jar.

Toasted coconut is prepared in the same way as Toasted Nuts (method follows).

COLOURED SUGAR CRYSTALS

Use either granulated sugar or roughly crushed sugar lumps and colour and dry in the same way as the coloured coconut above.

TOASTED NUTS

Whole flaked or chopped nuts may be lightly toasted to improve both colour and flavour. Almonds and hazelnuts are the most commonly used varieties.

To toast nuts, remove the rack from the grill pan and line the pan with a piece of foil. Spread the nuts over the foil. Heat the grill and toast the nuts under a medium heat, stirring occasionally until evenly browned. This will only take a few seconds. Lift out the foil carefully and leave the nuts to cool. This method may also be used to remove the skins from hazelnuts. Roast them under the grill, then rub the skins off while the nuts are still hot.

Toasted nuts are best used on the same day; alternatively, store when cold in a screw-topped jar for a few days.

PRALINE

This is a fine powder of crushed nuts and caramel used to flavour creams and fillings. Crushed roughly, it may be used as a cake decoration.

oil for greasing
50 g/2 oz caster sugar
50 g/2 oz almonds, toasted

Brush a baking sheet with oil. Place the sugar and nuts in a small, heavy-bottomed saucepan and heat slowly until the sugar melts, stirring occasionally. Continue cooking until the sugar turns from pale golden in colour to deep golden. Quickly pour the caramel on to the prepared baking sheet and leave until cold.

Crush the caramel to a fine powder with a rolling pin or pestle and mortar. Alternatively, break it up roughly and crush in a blender. Store the powder in a dry screw-topped jar for up to 3 months.

MAKES ABOUT 100 G/4 OZ

FROSTED FLOWERS AND LEAVES

Suitable flowers include freshly picked small, thin-petalled flowers such as primroses, sweet peas, violets and fruit blossom. Check that the selected flower is not poisonous if eaten. Suitable leaves include rose leaves, mint, sage and French parsley.

Prepare the flowers by gently shaking them upside down. Spread them out on absorbent kitchen paper. Leave for about 20 minutes to ensure any insects have crawled out. To prepare the leaves, gently swish through cold water. Shake dry and spread the leaves out on absorbent kitchen paper to dry. Frost at least three times as many flowers or leaves as you may require as they are very fragile.

1 egg white
caster sugar

In a bowl, lightly beat the egg white with 5 ml/1 tsp water until the egg is no longer stringy but not frothy. Using a fine paint brush, paint a thin layer of egg wash over and under the petals or leaves, being careful not to miss any part. Sprinkle them lightly all over with sugar until evenly coated. Spread the frosted flowers out on greaseproof paper or non-stick baking parchment.

Leave them to dry in an airy place away from direct sunlight until dry and hard. They can be easily removed from the paper.

Store the frosted flowers and leaves between sheets of tissue paper in a small cardboard box for up to several weeks. Check them occasionally and discard any that have crumpled.

SUGARED STRANDS

The thin coloured rind of most citrus fruits may be crystallised in thin strands to sprinkle over cakes and tarts. Lemon and orange are the fruits most frequently used.

1 orange or lemon
50 g/2 oz granulated sugar

Scrub the fruit with a small brush under running water. Using a potato peeler, shave off the peel in long, thin strips. With a small sharp knife, cut the peel into long, very fine strands. Place the strands in a small saucepan with 125 ml/4 fl oz water. Simmer for 2 minutes until the peel is tender. Remove strands with a slotted spoon and drain on absorbent kitchen paper.

Stir the sugar into the water and simmer over a low heat until melted. Increase the heat and boil rapidly, without stirring, until the syrup is reduced by half. Return the peel to the pan and cook, uncovered, until well glazed. Remove the peel with a slotted spoon and leave to cool on non-stick baking parchment. When cold, store the sugared strands in a box between leaves of waxed paper or non-stick baking parchment.

☀ **MICROWAVE TIP** The whole process may be done in the microwave using a suitable small bowl. Timings will be approximately the same but take care that the sugar does not brown too much. Check every 10 seconds once the syrup is boiling.

GRILLED TOPPINGS

These toppings are used on plain and light fruit cakes instead of icing and are spread over while the cake is still warm.

GOLDEN NUT TOPPING

50 g/2 oz butter, softened
100 g/4 oz soft light brown sugar
45 ml/3 tbsp single cream
100 g/4 oz chopped mixed nuts

Cream the butter and sugar together in a bowl, then beat in the cream and fold in the mixed nuts.

Spread the topping over the cake while it is cooling. Place the cake under a preheated low grill. Heat for 2-3 minutes until the topping is bubbling and light golden in colour. Leave the cake to cool before cutting.

SUFFICIENT TO COVER TWO 15 CM/6 INCH SQUARE CAKES

VARIATION

WALNUT TOPPING Use 100 g/4 oz chopped walnuts instead of mixed nuts.

GOLDEN COCONUT TOPPING

50 g/2 oz butter, softened
100 g/4 oz soft light brown sugar
75 g/3 oz desiccated coconut
45 ml/3 tbsp single cream

Combine the butter, sugar and coconut in a bowl and work ingredients together until well blended. Stir in the cream and spread the topping over the warm cake. Place the cake under a preheated low grill for 3-4 minutes until the topping is golden brown in colour. Leave to cool before cutting.

SUFFICIENT TO COVER TWO 15 CM/6 INCH SQUARE CAKES

VARIATION

ORANGE COCONUT TOPPING Use granulated sugar and orange juice instead of the brown sugar and cream.

MRS BEETON'S TIP Take great care when browning coconut under the grill, either on its own or in a topping. Do not have the grill too hot and watch the topping closely as it browns quickly and it may become scorched if it is left to cook unattended.

HEALTHIER ALTERNATIVES

Whether you are counting the calories or courting healthier eating habits, you may wish to use less sugar and fat in your recipes.

Sugar not only provides sweetness but also bulk, so this should be replaced with fruit, ground nuts or low-fat cream cheese. Butter may be replaced with vegetable oil-based spreads or low-fat cream cheese. Use plenty of natural flavourings or add a few drops of liqueur, and the results will be just as tasty as when conventionally made.

APRICOT SPREAD

8 apricot halves, canned in natural juice, drained
175 g/6 oz low-fat cream cheese
few drops of lemon juice

Purée or sieve the apricots. In a bowl, cream the cheese and lemon juice together and gradually beat in the apricot purée. Alternatively, place all ingredients in a blender or a food processor and work until the mixture is light and creamy. Chill the spread before use.

SUFFICIENT TO FILL A 20 CM/8 INCH CAKE

MRS BEETON'S TIP Fresh apricots or dried apricots may be substituted for canned. Soak dried apricots overnight and simmer in soaking liquor for 5-10 minutes.

APPLE AND BLACKCURRANT SPREAD

This is a thick fruit purée which may replace jam in a recipe. Because of its low sugar content, it will not keep for more than a week.

225 g/8 oz cooking apples, peeled and chopped
175 g/6 oz blackcurrants, topped and tailed
150 ml/¼ pint unsweetened apple juice
30 ml/2 tbsp apple concentrate
grated rind and juice of 1 orange

Combine the apples, blackcurrants and apple juice in a small saucepan. Cover and cook over a low heat until the fruit is soft, stirring occasionally.

Add the apple concentrate, orange rind and juice and simmer, uncovered, until the mixture is thick and pulpy. Stir occasionally to prevent the mixture from burning on the base. The purée is ready when the base of the saucepan can be seen as the mixture is stirred. Place the purée in a clean container, cover and when cold refrigerate for up to 1 week.

SUFFICIENT FOR TWO LAYERS IN ONE 18 CM/7 INCH CAKE

CITRUS CHEESE ICING

100 g/4 oz low-fat cream cheese
75 g/3 oz icing sugar, sifted
10 ml/2 tsp finely grated lemon or orange rind
30 ml/2 tbsp lemon or orange juice

Place cheese and sugar in a bowl and blend them together. Add rind and juice and beat all the ingredients together until light.

SUFFICIENT TO FILL A 20 CM/8 INCH CAKE

QUICK GUIDE TO USING COVERINGS, FILLINGS AND TOPPINGS WITH PLAIN CAKES

The following chart offers a quick-reference guide to using the recipes in this chapter with any type of cake you might bake.

	Small Cakes	Victoria Sandwich Cake	Sponge Cakes	Madeira Cake	Chocolate Cakes	Light Fruit Cakes	Rich Fruit Cakes	Cheese-cakes
GLAZES AND COATINGS								
Apricot Glaze	■	■		■		■	■	■
Chocolate Glaze	■	■	■		■			
Maraschino Glaze		■	■					■
Glaze for Sweet Flans			■					■
ALMOND PASTE AND MARZIPAN								
Marzipan				■		■	■	
Almond Paste				■		■	■	
Cooked Almond Paste				■		■	■	
BUTTER ICINGS AND FUDGE ICINGS								
Buttercream	■	■		■	■			
Rich Buttercream	■	■	■	■	■			
Fluffy Buttercream		■	■		■			
French Butter Icing		■	■		■			
Chocolate Fudge Icing	■				■			
Dark Fudge Icing	■	■			■			
GLACÉ ICINGS								
Glacé Icing	■	■	■	■	■			
Chocolate Glacé Icing					■			
Glacé Fondant	■	■	■	■				
FROSTINGS								
American Frosting		■	■	■	■			
Quick American Frosting		■	■	■	■			
Caramel Frosting		■	■	■				
Whipped Cream Frosting		■	■	■	■			
FONDANTS								
Traditional Fondant	■		■	■	■		■	
Quick Fondant	■		■	■	■		■	
Syrup-based Fondant	■		■	■	■		■	

	Small Cakes	Victoria Sandwich Cake	Sponge Cakes	Madeira Cake	Chocolate Cakes	Light Fruit Cakes	Rich Fruit Cakes	Cheese-cakes
ROYAL ICING								
Using egg white or dried egg white						■	■	
MOULDING ICINGS								
Sugar Paste	■	■		■		■	■	
Gelatine-based Sugar Paste	■	■		■		■	■	
Moulding Paste	■	■		■		■	■	
FILLINGS								
Rum and Walnut Filling		■	■		■			
Coconut Filling	■	■		■	■			
Cream Fillings		■	■		■			■
Custard Fillings		■	■		■			■
Confectioners' Custard		■	■					■
Confectioners' Custard with Brandy		■	■		■			■
Mock Cream		■	■		■			
Quick Diplomat Cream		■	■		■			■
TOPPINGS								
Toasted Nuts	■	■	■	■	■	■		■
Praline			■	■	■			■
Coconut	■	■		■				
Coloured Sugar Crystals				■		■		
Frosted Flowers and Leaves				■			■	
Sugar Strands	■	■	■					
GRILLED TOPPINGS								
Golden Nut Topping		■		■		■		
Golden Coconut Topping		■		■		■		
HEALTHIER ALTERNATIVES								
Citrus Cheese Icing	■	■	■		■			
Apricot Spread		■	■					
Apple and Blackcurrant Spread		■	■					

BASIC FILLING AND COVERING TECHNIQUES

Before progressing to piping designs of intricate detail, master the basic techniques in this chapter. From applying the first coat of glaze to achieving a perfect finish on a flat-iced cake, all the advice you need to ensure success is included here.

As with most skills, there are several ways of achieving the desired result; this is particularly true of cake decorating. In this chapter, the basic methods of filling and covering cakes are explained, using various recipes from the previous chapter. This first process of coating or covering forms the base for any decoration, simple or elaborate. Occasionally, an alternative method is given and it is a good idea to experiment with different methods to find out which suits you best.

The quality of the cake is important in determining the finished appearance. For example, the flatter the top of the cake, the better will be the final result. Make sure that you use the correct sized cake tin for the quantity of cake mixture, as peaked cakes are usually the result of using too small a tin for the mixture. Try to avoid slicing the top off a fruit cake; if this is not possible, never invert the cut side on to a cake board as this tends to draw the moisture out of the cake.

Before you begin to decorate a cake, make sure that you have all the equipment to hand and, if possible, choose a time when you are least likely to be disturbed until you have finished. Some icings set or stiffen quickly, so they need to be used efficiently without even a short break. The cake should be placed on a plate, board or wire rack, depending on the type of icing used. Use a dry pastry brush to brush away all loose crumbs which may spoil the icing.

A turntable is useful if you are coating the side of a round cake with icing. Alternatively, stand the cake on its board on a biscuit tin or upturned cake tin to raise the height of the cake and to make it easier to rotate. All the equipment must be scrupulously clean and the work surface must also be absolutely clean, dry and free of any specks of dust if the icing or cake covering is rolled out.

FILLING AND COVERING CAKES WITH APRICOT GLAZE

Apricot glaze can be used to sandwich cake layers together or it can be applied as a decorative coating. A variety of toppings can be sprinkled on to the glaze to complete the decoration. For example, try toasted, chopped or flaked nuts, toasted or coloured desiccated coconut, grated or flaked chocolate, finely chopped glacé fruits, chocolate vermicelli or praline. Before you begin, make sure that you have the following items prepared and close by ready to be used:

Apricot Glaze (page 20)
dry pastry brush
palette knife
the prepared topping (if used)
greaseproof paper or non-stick baking
    parchment
a plate or board for the completed cake

If not freshly prepared, re-heat the glaze with an additional 5 ml/1 tsp of water and bring it to the boil. Then leave it to cool a little but use it while still warm. Brush any loose crumbs from the top and sides of the cake. If you are adding a topping, have it prepared and spread it in a thick layer on a piece of greaseproof paper.

TO COAT THE SIDES OF THE CAKE

Quickly brush the glaze around the sides of the cake, making sure they are evenly coated. If using topping, place one hand on the top of the cake and the other under it, then lightly roll the cake in the topping until the sides are evenly covered. Press the cake down very lightly to coat the glaze thinly in topping. If too much topping is taken up at first, then the covering will be uneven and some areas will be sticky with glaze. Place the cake on a plate or board.

TO COVER THE TOP OF THE CAKE

Lightly brush the glaze over the top of the cake and sprinkle it liberally with topping. Lay a piece of clean greaseproof paper on top and press it down lightly to ensure that the coating sticks. Remove the paper.

FILLING AND TOPPING CAKES WITH BUTTERCREAM

Have the following items prepared and at hand before you begin:

the prepared cake
large serrated knife
Buttercream (page 24)
palette knife
plate or board for the completed cake

CUTTING THE CAKE INTO LAYERS

Place the cake on a flat surface and use a large serrated knife to slice horizontally through the cake, about 5 cm/2 inches in towards the centre. Slowly rotate the cake as you cut, then continue rotating and slicing the cake until it is sliced right through into two equal layers. Lift off the top layer and place it on a flat surface, top side uppermost.

TO FILL AND TOP THE CAKE

The buttercream should be of soft spreading consistency. If it was made in advance beat it to soften the mixture, adding a few drops of milk or fruit juice if necessary. Alternatively, the buttercream may be softened by warming in the microwave for 5 seconds on Defrost. Stiff icing is difficult to spread and it will drag the surface of the cake.

Use about one-third of the buttercream to sandwich the cake layers. Using a palette knife, lightly spread the buttercream evenly over the base layer of the cake, to within 5 mm/¼ inch of the edge. Carefully position the second cake layer on top. Spread the remaining buttercream on top of the cake in the same way. Finish the cake by smoothing the buttercream with the palette knife, then marking it with a fork or serrated scraper.

TO COAT THE SIDES OF THE CAKE

If the sides of the cake are covered with buttercream, divide the quantity of buttercream into four. Use one quarter for the filling, two quarters to cover the sides of the cake and the remaining quarter for the top. Spread the buttercream around the cake. The sides can be lightly rolled in a dry topping as when filling and covering with apricot glaze (see left).

If the top of the cake is to be covered in Glacé Icing (page 27), spread the buttercream up into a small ridge around the top edge of the cake to stop the icing spilling over the side.

COATING CAKES WITH GLACÉ ICING

This simple icing is not firm enough for piping or rolling. It is poured over the cake and allowed to set before any decoration is added. Glacé icing is usually only used on the top of a cake. When it dries, it is brittle and it tends to craze, especially if you move the cake before the icing is quite dry. The consistency of the icing should be similar to thick cream that will just flow to find its own level. It must not be so thin that it runs off the cake. Do not make the icing until you are ready to use it. There are two ways of coating the top of a cake with glacé icing.

Method 1 This method is used if the sides of the cake are coated with buttercream or a glaze and topping. The sides of the cake must be decorated first, taking care to extend the covering up along the top edge to form a small, even ridge.

Make up the glacé icing and pour it in a slow, steady stream starting at the centre of the cake and working in a circular movement towards the edge. The icing should find its own level but small areas may have to be teased towards the edge using the pointed end of a knife. Leave the icing to set, undisturbed, for several hours.

Method 2 If the sides of the cake are not covered, cut out a band of double-thick non-stick baking parchment to fit round the cake and extend about 1 cm/½ inch above the top edge. Place the collar in position so that it fits the cake tightly and secure it in place with a paper clip.

Make the icing and pour it on to the top of the cake as in Method 1. When the icing is dry, use a hot, dry knife to slice between the icing and the paper collar as you peel away the paper.

COATING CAKES WITH FROSTINGS OR FUDGE ICINGS

Most frostings have to be spread quickly over the cake as soon as they have been made or they will set in the bowl. It is, therefore, important to have the cake ready to ice before you begin. As they are spread on the cake, frostings and fudge icings begin to set, so it is not possible to pipe with them. Hot water is used to heat a palette knife for spreading the icing but the knife must be dried before use. It is essential to have everything organised before you begin to make the icing, so that it can be used immediately:

cake, ready-filled if required
plate or board
dry pastry brush
small palette knife
small quantity of hot water for heating the
    palette knife
any decorations or toppings
ingredients for frosting or fudge icing

Place the cake on a flat plate or board. Alternatively, rest it on an upturned plate so that when the icing has set, the cake can be transferred easily to its serving plate without the icing being touched and spoilt. Brush away any loose cake crumbs. Place the palette knife in the hot water. Make the icing, following the chosen recipe, and cover the cake immediately, using either of the methods that follow. Add any decorations to the cake before the icing sets.

FOR A SOFT FINISH

Pour all the icing on top of the cake and work quickly using the *dry*, hot knife. Draw the icing over the cake and down the sides, working in small circular movements from the centre outwards. Using a clean, hot knife, swirl the icing into peaks as it begins to set.

FOR A STIFFER ICING

First cover the sides of the cake. Spread about two-thirds of the icing round the sides, using the *dry*, hot knife and working quickly in small circular movements. Draw the icing up towards the top of the cake.

Spoon the remaining icing on the top of the cake and work quickly to draw the blobs of icing together to make an even coating. Use a clean, hot knife to quickly swirl the icing into soft peaks.

COVERING CAKES WITH TRADITIONAL FONDANT

Traditional fondant may be used as a cake covering when warmed and diluted with stock syrup. When dry it gives a smooth, shiny finish. It is most frequently used to coat small, fancy cakes such as petits fours. Fruit cakes must have a base coating of marzipan or almond paste before a coating of traditional fondant is applied. On a larger cake, it is essential that the surface is uncut and level, or the icing will flow away from the centre. Turn the cake upside down if necessary. Before you start, check through the following list, making sure that everything is ready:

Traditional Fondant (page 30)
basin
saucepan of hot water
wooden spoon
Stock Syrup (page 30) or boiled water
food colouring, if used
the prepared cake, or cakes
wire rack
baking sheet lined with non-stick baking
    parchment
dry pastry brush
Apricot Glaze (page 20)
small palette knife
small pointed knife

PREPARING THE FONDANT

Place the fondant in the basin over the saucepan of hot water and stir it occasionally until it has melted. Dilute the fondant to the consistency of thick cream by adding a little stock syrup or water. Add a few drops of food colouring at this stage, if used.

PREPARING THE CAKE

Place the cake on a wire rack and stand it over the lined baking sheet. Brush the cake with a dry brush to remove excess crumbs. Prepare the apricot glaze and brush it lightly over the cake. A small ball of marzipan may be placed in the centre of each cake when making petits fours.

COATING WITH FONDANT

When the fondant is ready, spoon it carefully over the cake and let it run down the sides to coat the cake completely. Use the pointed end of the knife to tease small areas of icing into place, if necessary, to ensure that the cake is evenly coated. Any fondant that drips through the rack can be collected and re-used, providing it is free from crumbs and glaze. Stir the fondant occasionally to prevent a skin from forming. Leave the fondant to set, then neaten the base of the cake by trimming away excess icing.

SWIRLED FONDANT

Alternatively, the icing can be applied more thickly and swirled with a knife as it sets.

COVERING CAKES WITH ALMOND PASTE OR MARZIPAN

Fruit cakes must be covered with almond paste or marzipan before they are coated with royal icing or covered with rolled-out icings or traditional fondant. The almond paste provides a flat surface for the icing and it also prevents the fruit in the cake from discolouring the icing. The cake covered with almond paste should be left in a dry place for at least a week, and up to two weeks for a wedding cake, before the icing is added. Lay a piece of greaseproof paper loosely over the top of the cake to protect it from dust. Never put the almond-paste-coated cake in an airtight tin or the paste will go mouldy.

For a professional finish, the surface must be as flat as possible. Even the flattest cake will need a little building up at the edge but if the cake is too domed, the almond paste will have to be very thick to compensate. When working, it is important to keep all crumbs away from the almond paste. Any that find their way on to the surface of the paste may discolour the icing. Assemble all the equipment and ingredients before you begin to work with the almond paste, and make sure that the work surface is scrupulously clean and dry. You will need:

the prepared cake or cakes
non-stick baking parchment
scissors
cake board
dry pastry brush
Apricot Glaze (page 20) or pure alcohol
   Almond Paste (page 22) or Marzipan
   (page 22)
sifted icing sugar for dusting surface
rolling pin
sharp knife
small palette knife
string
small spirit level (optional)
spacers (optional)

TO COVER THE TOP OF THE CAKE

There are two methods that can be used for covering the top of the cake with almond paste or marzipan. Method 2 is suitable for small and medium-sized cakes, but you may find method 1 easier when covering larger cakes, for example, the bottom tier of a large wedding cake.

Method 1 Cut a piece of parchment to fit the top of the cake exactly. To do this either measure the cake accurately or stand the cake on a piece of parchment and draw round it, then transfer the pattern to a clean

Method 1

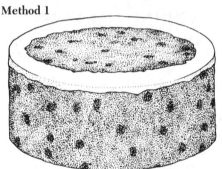

1 Press small rolls of paste around the edge of the cake to ensure the top is level.

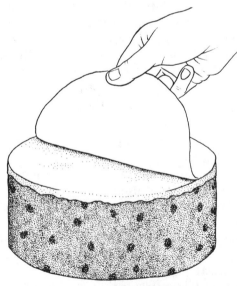

2 Invert the paper pattern and the paste on top of the cake, press lightly, then peel away the paper.

piece of parchment. Remember that if you draw round the tin in which the cake was cooked, you will need to cut slightly within the line to compensate for the thickness of the tin. Lightly dust the paper pattern with icing sugar.

Place the cake in the centre of the cake board and brush away all loose crumbs. Lightly glaze the top of the cake, around the outer edge only, with apricot glaze or alcohol.

Knead small pieces of almond paste and shape them into thin sausages. Place these all round the top outer edge of the cake. Holding the side firmly, with one hand extended to the height of the cake, press and mould the paste towards the centre of the cake to level the top. Lay a sheet of parchment on the top of the cake and roll it lightly with a rolling pin (do not use the paper pattern for this). Remove the parchment and brush the top of the cake with more glaze or alcohol.

Knead one-third of the remaining almond paste lightly into a ball and press it out on the centre of the paper pattern. Lightly dust the rolling pin with icing sugar and roll out the almond paste evenly, rotating the paper until the paste is even in thickness and the same size as the paper. If you have spacers, then use them to make sure that the paste is rolled out evenly. Trim the edges if necessary.

Lift up the paper pattern and the paste, then invert the paste on to the cake, positioning it carefully. Lightly press to stick the almond paste, then peel off the paper.

Method 2 Lightly dust the work surface with icing sugar and brush the top of the cake with apricot glaze or alcohol.

Lightly knead about one third of the paste and roll it out evenly, using spacers if available, to 2.5 cm/1 inch larger than the top of the cake. Invert the cake, glazed side downwards, on to the paste.

Using the palette knife, carefully work round the edge of the cake, pushing and easing the paste under the cake to fill the

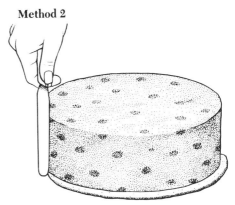

Method 2

Invert the cake on to the paste, then use a palette knife to ease the edges of the paste around the cake to make a level top.

gap. This ensures that the paste will be level.

Trim off any excess paste where necessary, then carefully turn the cake over, making sure that the almond paste is not left behind on the work surface. Centre the cake, paste-side uppermost, on the cake board.

TO COVER THE SIDES OF THE CAKE

Two alternative methods are given and they can be used with either almond paste or marzipan for all shapes of cake. Method 1 is the best to use for very large cakes.

Method 1 Measure the height of the cake accurately with a piece of string. Measure the circumference with string and add on 1 cm/ ½ inch to compensate for the thickness of the almond paste. From a sheet of parchment, cut a paper pattern that measures twice the height and half the circumference of the cake. Lightly dust the pattern with icing sugar. Brush the sides of the cake to remove all crumbs.

Lightly knead the remaining almond paste and shape it into a flat sausage the same length as the pattern. Place the paste down the middle of the paper pattern. Flatten the roll, then roll it out evenly across the width to fit the pattern exactly. Trim the edges, if necessary. With the sharp knife, cut the strip of paste in half along its length to make two equal strips, then following the same cutting line made by the knife, cut the paper in half with scissors.

Small Round Cakes Brush the side of the cake with apricot glaze or alcohol. Hold the top and bottom of the cake between the palms of your hands and position the side of the cake carefully on one piece of paste, then roll the cake along its length. Repeat with the second piece. Place the cake in the middle of the cake board, carefully peel off the paper and smooth the joins with a palette knife.

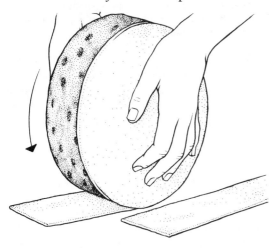

Large Round Cakes Position the cake in the middle of the cake board and brush apricot glaze or alcohol around the side. Lift up one strip of paste on the paper and place it in position around the cake. Repeat with the second piece. Carefully remove the paper and smooth the joins. Smooth around the cake with your hands to press the almond paste securely on to the cake.

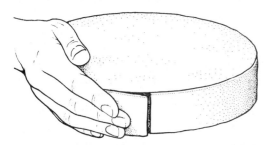

Square Cakes Attach the almond paste to a square cake as for the large round cake. It is easier if you avoid having the joins on the corners. Mould the corners neatly once the paste is in position and when the joins have been smoothed. For very large square cakes, divide each length of paste into two for easier handling.

Method 2 Position the cake in the centre of the board. Measure the height and circumference of the cake, then lightly brush the cake with apricot glaze or alcohol.

Dust the work surface with icing sugar, then lightly knead the remaining almond paste and roll it into a long, plump sausage. Flatten the paste and roll it into a strip that measures the same height as the cake, and the same length as the circumference of the cake. Trim the edges of the paste and roll it up loosely. Place one end of the roll on the cake and unroll the paste, pressing it firmly on to the side of the cake. Smooth the join together with a palette knife.

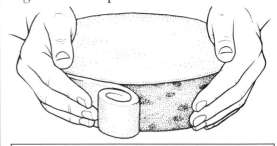

> 🍶 **MRS BEETON'S TIP** It is worth spending time on covering the cake smoothly with almond paste as it is difficult to compensate for unevenness when coating with icing. Check the level of your work surface with a spirit level before you begin – you may be surprised how much a surface can slope. Check the level of the cake when the top has been covered with paste and smooth out any uneven areas with a rolling pin, if necessary. There is no need to stick a fruit cake on to the cake board as the weight of mixture and finished icing will be sufficient to keep it in place.

COVERING CAKES WITH SUGAR PASTE AND MOULDING ICINGS

Rolled out icing can be applied directly on to a light cake. Fruit cakes should be covered with a layer of almond paste before the icing is placed on top, otherwise the icing will quickly discolour. If you dislike almond paste, try placing two layers of sugar paste over the cake, allowing the first layer to dry well before adding the second. This is not suitable for a wedding cake or any cake that is intended to be kept but for most other occasions you might get away with it.

Make sure that all your equipment is clean and free from grease. It is also a good idea to wear a large, clean apron, as small flecks of fluff from your clothing can easily fall on to the icing. Scrub the work surface and dry it thoroughly. Remove any rings from your fingers, as these would mark the icing when smoothing the surface on the cake. If you have long fingernails, take care not to mark the icing with them as you work. Impressions on the icing are difficult to eradicate.

Do not use cornflour for rolling out sugar paste that is to be placed directly on the cake as the starch will ferment. Use finely sifted icing sugar to lightly dust the work surface and the rolling pin. Cornflour can be used on the icing which is not directly in contact with a moist cake, for example to buff the top surface, for moulding flowers or making other decorations. Knead the paste lightly, using just the fingertips and use only a fine dusting of sugar. If you knead the paste too vigorously air pockets will be trapped and the surface will be uneven.

Choose a cool time of day to work and avoid using artificial light. Hairline cracks may not be seen until the morning when it will be too late to remove them. Similarly, colouring should be added to the paste in daylight. Remember, colours dry a shade or two darker.

TO COLOUR SUGAR PASTE

Remove a piece of paste about the size of a large walnut from the weighed-out quantity. Add a little paste colour to this small ball of icing and knead it in well. The ball will probably be several shades darker than required. Break off small pieces of the coloured paste and knead them lightly but thoroughly into the white paste, adding extra pieces of colour as required.

If you are matching the colour of the icing to a fabric or similar, break off a small piece, press it out thinly and leave it to dry for a few hours before checking the colour. Carefully wrap the remaining pieces of paste separately until required. When the required depth of colour has been obtained, break off a small piece and wrap it up well, keeping it, and any of the remaining deeply coloured ball, in case extra icing has to be coloured.

WORKING WITH SUGAR PASTE

Assemble all the ingredients and utensils before you begin to work on the cake:

cake, on a cake board
dry pastry brush
Apricot Glaze (page 20), alcohol or Butter-
    cream (page 24)
sifted icing sugar
rolling pin
spacers (optional)
knife
cornflour for buffing the icing

Measure the surface of the cake to be covered, including the depth of the side. Brush away all loose crumbs from the cake. If the cake is covered in almond paste, lightly coat it with apricot glaze or alcohol. Spread a thin layer of buttercream over a sponge or similar cake which is not covered in almond paste. Clean the board.

Lightly dust the work surface with icing sugar, then lightly knead the paste with the fingertips until it is smooth. Shape the ball of paste into the final shape required; for example shape a ball for a round cake, a box for a square cake or a sausage shape for a long thin strip of cake.

Lightly dust the rolling pin with icing sugar and roll out the paste evenly, using spacers, if available. The rolled out paste should be no thicker than 5 mm/¼ inch and it should be about 2.5 cm/1 inch shorter than required, as the icing will stretch and drop when it is hung over the edge of a cake. For example, if the cake to be covered is 20 cm/8 inches in diameter and 5 cm/2 inches deep, the paste should be rolled to a diameter of 28 cm/11 inches.

TO COVER A ROUND CAKE

Carefully slide the rolling pin under the paste, lift it up and position it accurately over the cake. With clean, dry hands, lightly dusted in cornflour, work the icing with the palm of your hand in a circular movement from the centre of the cake towards the edge. The icing will drop down the side and should

be lightly pressed and smoothed around the cake. Always work in a light, circular movement and avoid marking the icing with your fingernails. Trim the paste at the base of the cake, if necessary. You will probably find that you need to wash your hands again at this

stage. Ensure they are well dried, dust them very lightly with cornflour and quickly but lightly buff up the surface of the cake with the palm of one hand. Using both hands, one either side of the cake, buff up the side with small circular movements, rotating the cake as necessary.

TO MAKE A SHARPER TOP EDGE FOR PIPING

Do this before the final buffing. Using both hands, one to extend the icing on the side of the cake upwards slightly and the other to smooth the paste on the top of the cake, mould a sharp edge. This step is only necessary if you intend adding a piped edge around the cake.

TO COVER A SQUARE CAKE

Follow the instructions for covering a round cake but pay attention to the corners immediately you have laid the rolled out icing over the cake. Lift the icing and work it away from the corner, not towards it. Gently ease the paste back along the sides of the cake until it is smooth. You must do this at once, otherwise thick pleats form on the corners of the cake. Continue smoothing the icing as for the round cake, trimming the edges neatly and moulding sharp edges and corners.

Leave the cake to dry out at room temperature for at least 24 hours before adding any decoration, longer if possible. Cover the top with a piece of greaseproof paper when the surface is dry to protect it from dust.

TIERED CAKES

If you are decorating a tiered cake, follow the instructions on page 126 for setting on the pillars at this stage.

COATING CAKES WITH ROYAL ICING

This icing sets harder than any other icing and it is traditionally used for wedding cakes because it can support the weight of the tiers. Glycerine should not be added when the icing is used for tiered cakes because it softens the icing. Royal icing made with albumen or albumen substitutes tends to set harder than icing made with fresh egg white. Royal icing gives sharper edges and corners than the moulding icing or softer icings. This is better for piping a border or for adding an edging as decoration.

Royal icing can only be applied to firm cakes that are covered with almond paste or marzipan and have a firm, flat surface on which to apply icing. Make sure the almond paste or marzipan is completely dry before applying the icing. When working on a single cake, or one layer of a tiered-cake allow a minimum of 3 days to ice the cakes plus one week for the icing to dry. Allow 2 weeks or more for the icing on a tiered cake to dry.

WORKING WITH ROYAL ICING

For a good finish, three coats of royal icing should be applied; the final coat gives no thickness but makes a smooth, fine surface. Make up the full quantity of icing for all the cakes to be covered and mix the icing to a soft-peak consistency. Leave the icing to stand, covered, for 3-4 hours to dispel air bubbles.

After applying the first coat, carefully scrape the remaining icing into a clean bowl taking care that no particles of dried icing from the sides of the bowl are included. Cover the icing with a damp cloth and wrap the whole bowl in a polythene bag. The next day the icing will be a little slacker; give it a quick beat before applying it to the cake. Store the icing as before. Again, the icing will be slightly slacker for the next application.

Do not thicken the icing to the original consistency as thinner coats give a smoother finish.

It is important not to allow even one dried particle of icing to mix with the soft icing as this, when dragged across the cake, will leave a trail. If you do have particles of dried icing in the soft icing, then press it through a very fine, clean, nylon sieve. Keep the icing covered at all times with a clean, damp cloth.

Before starting, check that the work surface is level. When icing the top of the cake, the correct height is one at which you can stand with your arm bent at the elbow and your lower arm parallel to the cake.

Stand with your feet slightly apart, with one foot in front of the other. When you begin levelling the cake, start with the pressure on your front foot and gradually transfer this to the other foot as you draw the ruler across the top of the cake towards you. You will find that this enables you to complete the action with even pressure, and in one continuous movement.

Practise this position before you begin to ice the cake. Wear a large, clean apron as small flecks of fluff, hairs or specks of dust easily find their way from clothes on to the icing. If possible, ice the cake in daylight and choose a time when you are unlikely to be disturbed. Stand the cake board on a damp cloth or rubber mat to prevent it from slipping. Assemble all the equipment and ingredients that you will need before you begin to ice the cake:

marzipanned cake on board
Royal Icing (page 32), mixed to soft-peak
   consistency
large palette knife
small palette knife
clean damp cloth
ruler
scraper
small sharp knife (not serrated)
turntable (for a round cake)
glass-headed stainless steel pin

TO FLAT ICE THE TOP OF A ROUND OR SQUARE CAKE

Lightly beat the icing and place about half in the centre of the cake. Using the large palette knife, work the icing backwards and forwards, spreading it across the cake to cover the almond paste or marzipan. Pay particular attention to the edges and corners. Use the palette knife flat on the cake and press quite hard to break any air bubbles in the icing as you work. There is no need to use a hot knife unless your icing is too stiff. Never use a wet knife as the water will make the icing brittle.

Hold the ruler with both hands and position it at the back of the cake at an angle of 45 degrees. Ensure that the ruler is parallel to the cake at both ends. Position your feet correctly and with a firm, quick movement, draw the ruler across the cake towards you. Lift the ruler off sharply and

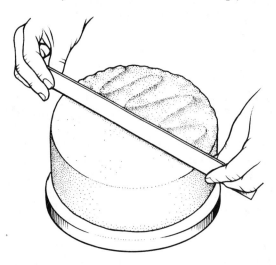

scrape the excess icing into the bowl; then cover the bowl of icing again.

If necessary, give the cake a quarter turn and repeat the process with a clean ruler. Using the sharp knife, scrape away the excess icing from the edge of the cake to give a clean sharp edge; discard this trimmed icing – do not return it to the bowl. Use a pin to prick any air bubbles that are visible on the

surface of the icing. Leave the cake to dry for 4–5 hours or more before icing the sides.

 MRS BEETON'S TIP Be confident and quick with the ruler. A slow, hesitant movement will result in a ridged effect in the icing.

TO ICE THE SIDE OF THE CAKE

Round Cake Place the cake on the turntable positioning it on a damp cloth, if necessary, to ensure that the board does not slip. Using the small palette knife, spread the icing evenly around the cake, making sure that you draw it up to the top edge. Position your left hand as far round the back of the turntable as possible so that it can be fully turned in one movement. Hold the scraper in the right hand parallel to the side of the cake and at an angle of 45 degrees. Rotate the turntable at an even speed, keeping regular pressure on the scraper until just before you reach the point at which you started, when you should slightly ease the pressure, then sharply pull away the scraper. Make sure that you move the turntable, not the scraper. Repeat a second time, if necessary, with a clean scraper, then trim off excess icing at the top edge, holding the blade parallel to the top of

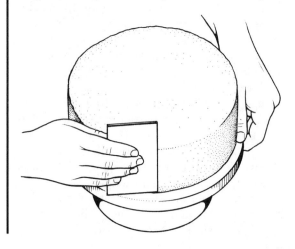

the cake. Using a pin, immediately prick any air bubbles that appear in the icing.

Square Cake Ice two opposite sides at a time, leaving them to dry for 4-6 hours before icing the remaining two sides.

Spread the icing on the side, paying particular attention to the top edge and corners. Hold the scraper parallel to the cake at an angle of 45 degrees and start at the back

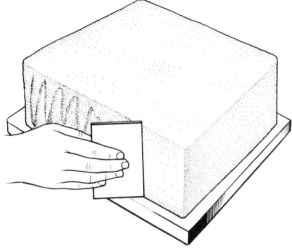

of the cake, drawing the scraper with a firm, even pressure towards you. Repeat a second time, if necessary, with a clean scraper, then scrape off the excess icing on the top edge and at the corners. Repeat this process on the opposite side.

SECOND OR THIRD COATS

Leave the first layer of icing to dry for 24 hours in a dry, cool place before adding a second layer. The same techniques should be used for each application of icing.

> **MRS BEETON'S TIP** Royal icing will not dry in a damp atmosphere. If the room is too hot, the almond paste or marzipan may sweat and discolour the icing.

TIPS FOR SUCCESS WITH ROYAL ICING

■ Make sure that all equipment is spotlessly clean before you begin as any tiny particles of dust or dirt will spoil the icing.

■ Always thoroughly sift the icing sugar before making the icing.

■ Make sure that the icing is well beaten and free of lumps before applying it to the cake.

■ Check the consistency of the icing before use, making sure that it is neither too soft or too stiff for spreading or piping.

■ Keep the icing sealed in an airtight container to prevent it drying out when it is not being used.

■ Avoid getting any particles of dry icing into the container of soft icing.

■ Leave layers of icing to dry thoroughly before adding another coating to the cake.

SIMPLE CAKE DECORATING TECHNIQUES

Presentation is always important when serving food, sweet or savoury, to give pleasure as well as to whet the appetite. In this chapter you will find lots of clever ideas and simple designs for decorated cakes. They are all fairly quick to complete and they do not demand years of experience or highly developed skills to ensure success. The finished decorations are all attractive and tasteful – ideal for anyone who is in the early stages of learning the fulfilling craft of cake decorating.

DECORATING CAKES WITH APRICOT GLAZE OR JAM

Apricot Glaze (page 20) or warmed and sieved jam can be used as a base for adding finishing touches to light sponge cakes. There are a few quick and easy ideas.

DOILY DESIGN

Coat the sides of the cake in glaze and roll in chopped nuts, desiccated or long-thread coconut, or grated chocolate. Lay a paper doily on top of the cake (or fold a circle of paper and cut out a series of shapes to make your own pattern). Place a little icing sugar in a small sieve and gently sift it over the doily on the cake, moving the sieve all over the cake to make an even layer of sugar. Using both hands, carefully lift the doily straight upwards off the cake.

ALMOND PASTE AND APRICOT GLAZE DECORATION

Roll out a piece of almond paste to fit around the sides of the cake (page 60). Brush the sides of the cake with apricot glaze and press the almond paste into position. Cut a circle of paper to fit the top of the cake, fold it in half and roll out a piece of almond paste to fit the semi-circle, then cut the paste into four equal wedges.

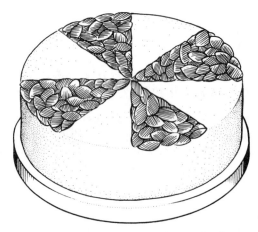

Spread the top of the cake with glaze and place the wedges of almond paste on top leaving alternate gaps of glaze. Sprinkle the wedges of glaze with toasted flaked almonds if you like.

DECORATING WITH PIPED BUTTERCREAM OR WHIPPED CREAM

Keep your hands as cool as possible when piping with buttercream or whipped fresh cream. Warm hands holding the piping bag can cause the cream to melt or become runny because of the butterfat content. Keep the kitchen cool and only fill the icing or piping bag one third full; start again with a fresh bag if the icing or cream does begin to melt. Chill the icing and cream before you start; alternatively, spoon the cream or icing into the icing bag and put the bag in the refrigerator for 10 minutes before using it.

If you want to cover a large area, for example, when decorating novelty cakes, use a large piping bag fitted with a savoy star nozzle (page 19). Avoid using a nylon bag, if possible, as these tend to make the icing or cream sweat. Do not hold the bag in the palms of your hands but squeeze it from the top. If you do need to support the bag, use only the fingers of your other hand and place them near the nozzle. If you are piping over a small area of the cake, for example around the base or the sides, use a double thickness paper icing bag (page 18) with a large nozzle.

Because buttercream and whipped cream are soft, the amount of pressure used will determine the size of the decoration. Use only light pressure, otherwise the stars will be too thick and you may run out of icing or cream before you have finished. It is best to have extra buttercream or whipped cream. If you are piping small areas have about one third more than you need; allow two thirds extra when piping over large areas of cake.

DECORATING WITH BUTTERCREAM

Unless otherwise stated, these designs may be used on any shape of cake.

FORK PATTERNS

Spread the sides of the cake with buttercream and roll them in chopped nuts, desiccated coconut or grated chocolate. Cover the top of the cake with buttercream; use a palette knife to smooth it over, then use a fork to mark a decorative pattern.

STRIPED-TOP CAKE

Roll out almond paste to fit the sides of the cake (page 60). Brush the sides with glaze (page 54) and press on the almond paste. Spread the top of the cake thinly with buttercream. Divide the remaining buttercream in half, colour each portion differently with food colouring and place them in separate icing bags fitted with star nozzles. Pipe lines of one colour across the top of the cake, leaving room for another line of icing

between each row. Pipe lines of the contrasting colour between the first rows of piping.

SCRAPER DESIGN

Cover the top of the cake with buttercream; smooth it over. Spread buttercream around the sides of the cake. Mark a comb pattern

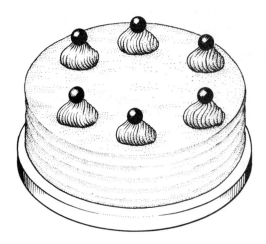

round the side, using the serrated edge of a scraper. Hold the scraper at an angle of 45 degrees and rotate the cake. If you have not got a turntable place the cake on a small biscuit tin or similar so that it is easier to rotate the cake. Use a fork or scalded, new hair comb if you do not have a scraper.

Put the remaining buttercream in a large icing bag fitted with a savoy star nozzle and pipe six or eight large swirls on the top of the cake. Alternatively, use two teaspoons to shape neat blobs of buttercream on the cake. Top each swirl with a nut, a piece of glacé cherry or a small sweet.

MUSHROOM CAKE

This is a clever idea for a round cake. Roll out a strip of almond paste to fit the side of the cake plus 1 cm/½ inch wider (page 60). Spread chocolate or pink buttercream thickly over the top of the cake and thinly around the side. Using a fork, mark the icing on the top of the cake from the edge, towards the

centre to represent the 'gills' of a mushroom. Press the almond paste on to the side of the cake and fold the top edge neatly, and loosely, down over the buttercream. Mould a small piece of almond paste to represent a stalk and dip the end in drinking chocolate powder. Position the stalk, brown end uppermost, in the centre of the cake.

For a child's birthday cake, cut out small

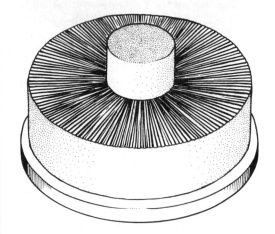

circles of red almond paste and stick them on to the side with a little jam or buttercream.

This design also works well with small cakes.

TWO-COLOUR STAR CAKE

Spread the side of a round cake thinly with buttercream and roll it in grated chocolate or chocolate vermicelli. Spread the top of the cake thinly with buttercream.

Divide the remaining buttercream between two basins and colour them as you wish; for example add melted chocolate or brown colouring to one portion and yellow to the second, or colour one portion pink and the second portion green. Place one portion in an icing bag fitted with a large star nozzle and pipe a circle of stars in the centre of the

Spread the sides with buttercream and draw a fork from the base upwards all round to mark a pattern in the cream on the side.

Place the remaining cream in a bag fitted with a large star nozzle and gently pipe small stars on the top of the cake to divide it into six or eight segments. Pipe a row of stars around the edge of the cake. If you like, sprinkle different, small decorations into each segment, for example hundreds and thousands, chocolate vermicelli, sprinkles or chopped nuts.

cake. Pipe two rows of stars in the same colour round the edge of the cake. Put the second portion of buttercream in a clean bag fitted with the same size nozzle. Pipe stars to fill in the top of the cake and pipe a row of stars round the lower edge of the cake. This simple decoration can be adapted to suit a square cake by piping a square of stars in the centre, then piping the edge and filling in.

SIMPLE BIRTHDAY CAKE

Spread buttercream evenly over the top and sides of the cake and use a fork or the serrated edge of a scraper to mark a vertical pattern up the sides. Clean the scraper or fork and mark a pattern across the top of the cake. Place the remaining buttercream in a bag fitted with a large star nozzle and pipe stars around the top and bottom edges of the

PIPED STAR DESIGN

Another idea for decorating a round cake. Spread buttercream thinly over the surface and use a palette knife to smooth it over.

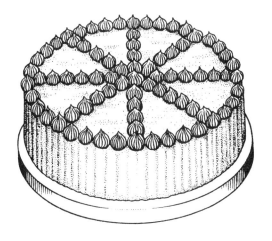

cake. Place buttercream in a contrasting colour, in an icing bag fitted with a plain nozzle and write 'Happy Birthday' on top of the cake. Alternatively, bought decorations can be put on top of the cake instead of writing.

SIMPLE DESIGNS USING WHIPPED CREAM

Whipped fresh cream can be used in the same way as buttercream but take care not to over-handle the piping bag and always work in a cool place. Unless otherwise stated, these designs may be used on any shape of cake.

CHOCOLATE SCROLL CAKE

Spread cream thinly over the top of the cake and thickly around the side. Comb the side using a scraper with a serrated edge held at an angle of 45 degrees to the cake. Rotate the cake, either using a turntable or by placing the cake on a small cake tin which makes it easier to turn. Use a fork if you do not have a scraper. Cover the top of the cake with a generous pile of chocolate scrolls (page 118).

SKEWER PATTERN

Spread cream over the top and sides of the cake and use a palette knife to smooth the top as neatly as possible. Spread cocoa powder or instant coffee powder over a piece of paper and lay a long, plain metal skewer in it. Press the skewer across the cake to mark diagonals. Wash, dry and re-dip the skewer as necessary. Press chocolate curls (page 118) or chocolate finger biscuits around the side of the cake. An excellent design for square cakes.

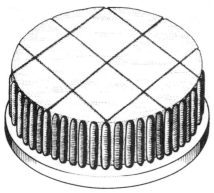

GLACÉ FRUITS AND CREAM

Spread the top of the cake thinly with cream. Spread cream thickly on the sides and use a fork or serrated scraper to mark a vertical

pattern in the cream. Pipe small stars of cream around the top edge and across the cake to divide it into six equal segments. Fill each segment with mixed finely chopped glacé fruits. This design works best on a round cake, but a square cake could be divided into blocks and filled in the same way.

CHOCOLATE ALMOND CAKE

Spread cream around the sides of the cake and roll it in toasted flaked almonds. Spread

cream over the top of the cake and use a palette knife to smooth it over. Drizzle melted chocolate over the top (page 116).

SIMPLE DECORATIONS USING GLACÉ ICING

FEATHER ICING

This is an attractive technique using coloured glacé icing. The colours and basic design can be varied but first follow the instructions for the basic method. Remember that the icing and decoration must be completed before the icing sets. Melted chocolate can be used instead of an icing in a contrasting colour (page 116).

Make the icing and brush any crumbs off the cake. Place 30 ml/2 tbsp of the icing in a small basin and add a few drops of food colouring to contrast with the main colour. Place the coloured icing in a paper icing bag (page 18). You do not need a nozzle.

Feather Icing

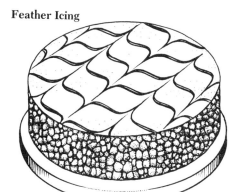

Fan Feather Icing

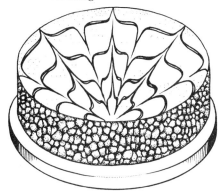

Use the main batch of icing to cover the top of the cake (page 56). Snip a small corner off the icing bag and immediately pipe lines of coloured icing across the cake about 1 cm/½ inch apart. Using a skewer or the point of a knife, draw lines across the piped coloured icing at 1 cm/½ inch intervals. Draw the skewer alternately in opposite directions. The coloured icing will sink into the main icing and it will drag into an attractive pattern as the skewer is drawn through it, creating the feathered effect.

Circular Feather Icing

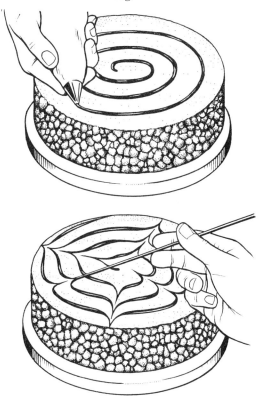

CIRCULAR FEATHER ICING

Instead of piping lines across a round cake, pipe circles at even distances out from the centre. Alternatively the circles can be piped to radiate out from one side like a fan (this works well on square cakes). Drag the icing with the skewer to create the feather effect.

SIMPLE DECORATIONS USING FONDANT

Traditional fondant thinned with stock syrup is too soft to use for elaborate piping or for swirling but it may be used as a pouring icing and can also be drizzled thinly over cakes for simple decorative effect. When decorating large cakes, the fondant should be poured over the top after the sides have been coated in another covering, for example apricot glaze and chopped nuts. Coat the sides of the cake in the chosen glaze and topping. Pour most of the fondant over the top of the cake and keep the extra warm. When the fondant on the cake is almost set, add a few drops of colouring to the warm fondant and place 30 ml/2 tbsp of it in a small, paper icing bag (page 18). Snip off just the point to make a very small hole and quickly drizzle the coloured fondant backwards and forwards across the top of the cake.

FEATHERED FONDANT

A feathered effect can be made by piping on the icing when the base coat is still wet and following the instructions for feathering glacé icing (page 71).

PLAIN FONDANT TOPPING

Coat the sides of the cake with a strip of almond paste (page 60) and pour fondant over the top of the cake. When the fondant has set, pipe small stars of whipped cream or buttercream around the edge.

FONDANT-COATED CAKE

Cover the top and sides of the cake in fondant (page 57). Piped chocolate motifs (page 116) can be added as simple decoration around the top of the cake. For a birthday cake use numerals denoting the age of the person as the shape for the chocolate motifs.

DECORATING CAKES WITH ALMOND PASTE OR MARZIPAN

Either almond paste or marzipan may be used as the main ingredient for cake decorations. Paste or marzipan may be coloured or moulded. Unless otherwise stated, the designs that follow may be used on any shape of cake.

TO COLOUR ALMOND PASTE OR MARZIPAN

Use a paste food colouring to avoid making the mixture sticky. Lightly knead the colour into the almond paste or marzipan on a work surface dusted with icing sugar. Take care not to overhandle it or it will become oily.

PLAITED-BASE CAKE

Cover the top and sides of the cake with almond paste or marzipan (page 58). Use a modelling tool or fork to press a design around the top edge of the cake. Place a plait of almond paste or marzipan around the base

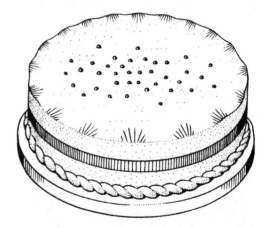

of the cake (see sugar paste ropes, twists and plaits, page 74). Sprinkle coloured sugar balls over the top of the cake and gently press them into the paste with a palette knife.

RIBBON WEAVE DESIGN

Cover the sides of the cake with roughly chopped nuts or toasted flaked almonds. Brush the top of the cake generously with apricot glaze.

Roll out almond paste or marzipan thickly and cut it into 1 cm/½ inch wide strips. Arrange two strips in a cross shape on top of the cake. Lay two more strips on the cake, one above and one below the first strip, leaving about 1 cm/½ inch between the strips.

Place two strips in the opposite direction, interweaving them with the previous two strips. Continue adding strips of paste, interweaving them until the surface of the

cake is completely covered. Trim the ends of the strips all round the edge of the cake. A colourful design can be achieved by using different coloured strips.

CRYSTAL FRUIT TOPPING

Roll out a strip of almond paste or marzipan to fit the sides of the cake. Use a modelling tool, fork or potato peeler to press out a pattern evenly over the paste. Brush the sides of the cake with apricot glaze and place the strip of almond paste in position.

Brush the top of the cake with apricot glaze, then cover it with a mixture of roughly chopped coloured glacé fruits, such as yellow, green and red cherries, mixed peel and crystallised ginger. Roll small balls of almond paste or marzipan and place them around the top edge of the cake.

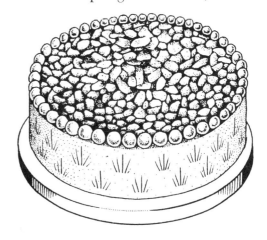

POINSETTIA CAKE

Cover the top and sides of the cake with almond paste or marzipan coloured pale green. Using red-coloured almond paste or marzipan, cut out small oval petal shapes for the sides and larger ones for the top of the cake. Use a little apricot glaze to stick the

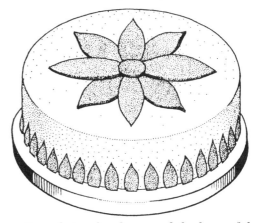

small petals in a border round the base of the cake. Overlap the large petals on the top to form a flower, again keeping them in place with a little apricot glaze. Cut a tiny circle of red almond paste to neaten the centre of the flower and place it in position.

SIMPLE DECORATIONS USING SUGAR PASTE

This is a wonderfully versatile icing which can be used to smooth-ice a cake or it can be moulded into simple decorations such as ropes, figures, plaques and flowers. It is also an invaluable ingredient for making novelty cakes. Here are some simple ideas; more complicated moulding techniques are explained later.

COVERING THE CAKE BOARD

Although cake boards are attractive, sometimes the soft line of a cake covered with sugar paste is enhanced if the icing extends to the edge of the board. The board can be covered in one operation when covering the cake but it is easier and neater to apply the icing to the board separately. The sugar paste should be rolled out and smoothed with a little cornflour. The measurements given are for a board which is 5 cm/2 inches larger than the cake. When the icing is completely dry, neaten the board by placing a strip of board edging or ribbon around it.

TO COVER A ROUND BOARD

Measure the circumference of the cake with string and divide the result by two if the cake is a small one, or by three or four if the cake is large. Centre the cake on the board.

Roll out pieces of sugar paste to the required lengths and make them 3 cm/1¼ inches wide. Place one strip on the cake board, butting one edge neatly up to the base of the cake. Gently ease the paste around the curve. Repeat with the remaining strip or strips, butting the joins together neatly, then smoothing them out with a palette knife. Trim off the excess paste at the edge of the board.

TO COVER A SQUARE BOARD

Place the square cake on the board. Roll out a strip of paste 3 cm/1¼ inches wide and the same length as one side of the board. Place the strip on the board, butting one edge neatly against the cake. Repeat with the remaining sides, loosely overlapping the paste at the corners.

Using a sharp knife, cut firmly and neatly diagonally from each corner of the cake to the corner of the board. Remove excess paste by gently lifting up the corners. Smooth the join with a palette knife or make it a feature by piping small stars or dots along it. Trim off excess paste at the edges of the board.

ROPES, TWISTS AND PLAITS

These are quick, simple edges which can be used to neaten the base of any cake; regardless of shape. They can be applied at the same time as covering the cake or later, when the paste has dried, in which case a little alcohol or cooled boiled water should be used to stick the edging to the cake.

Rope Measure the circumference of the cake and divide the total into two or four depending on the size of the cake. Small cakes can be edged with one piece of paste.

Lightly dust the work surface and your hands with cornflour and mould about 25 g/1 oz of sugar paste into a fat sausage. Place both hands over the middle of the roll, with your index fingers side by side. Using the pressure from the base of the fingers, especially the index fingers, begin rolling the paste backwards and forwards and at the same time gradually move your hands away from each other until a long, evenly thick rope is formed. The rope should be at least the required length plus 5 cm/2 inches and about 5 mm/¼ inch thick.

Twist Roll two ropes and loosely twist them together.

Twist

Plait

Plait Roll three ropes slightly thinner than 5 mm/¼ inch and loosely plait them together.

TO FIX THE EDGE ON TO THE CAKE

Lay the piece of rope around the base of the cake, taking care not to stretch it. Press it lightly on to the cake, brushing it first as you work with a little alcohol or boiled water, if necessary. Leave 2.5 cm/1 inch loose at each end. Fix any remaining pieces in place. Join the ropes by loosely twisting them together in a decorative manner; loose ends can be draped on the board or trimmed.

COLOURED EDGES

Colour the rope a contrasting colour to the main sugar paste. The twists and plaits can be made in two or more different colours.

MRS BEETON'S TIP Before fixing the ropes on to the cake, decide which is be the front so that the joins can be positioned either at the side or at the back and front.

CUT OUT SHAPES

Cut out sugar paste shapes are a simple and effective means of decorating cakes coated in sugar paste. They stick well on both dried and freshly rolled paste.

Colour the sugar paste as required and use the reverse side of a laminex board as a surface for rolling, if possible. Alternatively, dust a clean, dry, smooth work surface with a little cornflour. Use a small, clean, smooth rolling pin.

Using cutters Roll out the paste evenly to about the same thickness as short crust pastry. Stamp out shapes sharply and peel away excess paste. Slide a palette knife under the paste shape and lift it on to its position on the cake. With fingertips lightly dusted with cornflour, smooth the shape on to the cake using a small, circular movement.

Using a template Draw the required shape and cut it out in thin, white card. Roll out the sugar paste and lightly dust the surface with cornflour. Lay the template on the paste and cut around it with a small pointed knife. Take care not to press too heavily on the template or it may stick to the icing. Remove the template and peel away the excess paste. Lift the shape and smooth it on to the cake as above.

USING MODELLING TOOLS

Modelling tools, available from cake decorating suppliers, can only be used on sugar paste or similar icings when still soft, so mark the pattern in the icing as soon as you have covered the cake smoothly. A variety of tools are available to create different designs. Simply press the selected tool firmly into the sugar paste, then draw it up sharply to make a neat indentation. If the tool tends to stick to the icing, lightly dust it with cornflour.

Specialist marking tools are not essential for creating patterns. With a little imagination forks, vegetable peelers, spoon handles, pointed knives and other similar objects may also be used to create attractive patterns.

PATTERNS MADE WITH CRIMPERS

Crimpers are used to press designs around the edge of the soft paste. Several different designs are available. You do need to practise the technique on a thick piece of sugar paste if you are a novice at this type of decorating. Mistakes made directly on the cake are difficult to erase. If you do make a mistake, smooth over the icing with your fingertips, working in a circular movement.

To regulate the space between the crimpers, place an elastic band about 2.5 cm/1 inch from the open end so that the ends are fixed about 5 mm/¼ inch apart. Dip the ends of the crimpers in icing sugar or cornflour during use to prevent them sticking to the paste. Before starting, use a pin to prick a line around the cake to ensure that you mark the pattern in a straight line.

Press the crimpers into the icing, then gently pinch them together until the paste between the crimpers is 3 mm/⅛ inch thick. Re-open the crimpers to the fixed gap of 5 mm/¼ inch before lifting them away. It is very important to release the pressure and open the crimpers slightly *before* lifting them away or the paste may lift away with them.

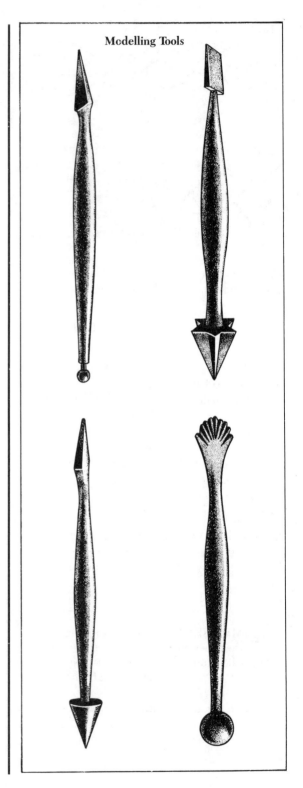

Modelling Tools

INSERTING RIBBON INTO SUGAR PASTE

The aim when attaching ribbon to a cake by this method is to give the impression that the ribbon is woven into the icing. The ribbon must be attached as soon as the cake is covered with sugar paste and while the icing is still soft. Take care not to mark the soft icing with your knuckles or fingernails as you work. If you wait until the icing has set, the ribbon will not readily stick into the slots.

Choose a narrow, satin ribbon which contrasts with the colour of the main icing. Ribbon which is a few shades darker looks best; remember that the sugar paste will be slightly darker when it is dry. Buy sufficient ribbon to go around the cake at least one and a quarter times. Cut the ribbon into 2 cm/¾ inch lengths and place these on a clean saucer.

Before you begin, cut a strip of clean greaseproof paper that equals the height of the cake and extends beyond the circumference by at least 5 cm/2 inches. Measure up from the bottom of the paper to the position where the ribbon is to be inserted and make pencil marks at 1 cm/½ inch intervals along the length of the paper. Assemble all equipment and ingredients before you start to cover the cake with paste:

cake on its board
Sugar Paste (page 42)
cornflour for buffing
ribbon pieces
ribbon insertion tool or a metal nail file
2 glass-headed pins
paper pattern

Cover the marzipanned cake with sugar paste (for quantities, see Chart, page 42) and buff the surface (page 62). Position the cake on a cake tin and sit down so that the cake is at eye level.

Lightly dust the paper pattern with cornflour and place it around the cake securing it in place with a pin at the back.

Prick out the position of the ribbon design on to the cake, then carefully remove the pattern. Smooth over any other marks which you may have made on the cake.

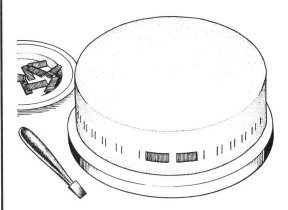

Cut vertical slits the same width as the ribbon around the cake at the marked 1 cm/½ inch intervals. Do this with a special ribbon insertion tool or the rounded, blunt end of a sterilised metal nail file. Be careful not to cut too deeply, or you will pierce right through to the almond paste or marzipan.

Start at the back of the cake and use the tool or file to press one end of a piece of cut ribbon into a slit. Leaving a small loop, insert the other end into the next slit. Leave a 1 cm/½ inch gap and insert the next piece of ribbon into the following slit. Continue around the cake.

The slits can be decorated with small piped beads or embroidery (pages 81 and 83). Small narrow strips of ribbon can be used in the same way to highlight a pattern made with crimpers.

MRS BEETON'S TIP Instead of cutting all the slits around the cake at the same time you may prefer to cut each slit as you insert the ribbon, at least for the first few lengths, so that you are sure that the spacing is correct for the cake.

SIMPLE DESIGNS USING SUGAR PASTE

These simple designs (see diagrams) are suitable for round or square cakes. Any home-made or shop-bought moulding icing can be used instead of sugar paste.

MODELLING TOOL DESIGN

Cover the top and the sides of the cake with sugar paste and mark a pattern around the top edge with a modelling tool. Place a single

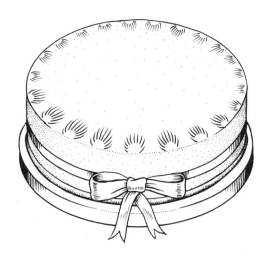

rope of sugar paste around the base of the cake and finish with a band of ribbon tied in a large bow.

CRIMPER DESIGN

Cover the top and the sides of the cake with sugar paste and use crimpers to mark a pattern around the top edge. Place a twisted rope of sugar paste around the base of the cake and a band of ribbon above. Add a bought greetings plaque or other decoration

to the top of the cake. Alternatively, cut out an appropriate numeral from rolled-out sugar paste in a contrasting colour.

BALLOON CAKE

Cover the top and the sides of the cake with sugar paste. Cover the board with paste. Cut

a template of a teddy bear, then cut out the shape in coloured sugar paste and position it on the cake. Cut balloons from paste in contrasting colours and position them around the cake. When the sugar paste is dry, use coloured icing pens to draw the string from the balloons to the teddy. Finish the cake by tying a narrow ribbon around its base.

SIMPLE TECHNIQUES FOR ROYAL ICING

Royal icing does not have to be smoothed over the cake to give a flat finish. It can be swirled and peaked to give a snow scene effect or it can be combed to create various designs.

SIMPLE SILK FLOWER CAKE

Cover the top and the sides of the cake with tinted sugar paste. Place a plaited rope of paste, tinted a slightly deeper colour, around the base of the cake. Decorate the cake with a small spray of silk flowers.

PEAKED ICING

The icing should be of soft-peak consistency (page 41), so that the tip of the peak just falls. Spread the icing thickly over the cake. Using a small palette knife, press it firmly into the icing and quickly draw it towards you by about 2 cm/¾ inch before pulling it sharply away from the icing and flicking it towards the back of the cake to form a soft swirly peak of icing. Move the cake around making random peaks all over the surface.

NIGHT SKY CAKE

Cover the side of the cake with apricot glaze and dark chocolate vermicelli. Cover the top

of the cake with sugar paste coloured midnight blue. Trim the edges neatly. Cut out small stars and a moon from yellow sugar paste and place them in position on the top of the cake.

COMBED ICING

A turntable is useful for this method of neatening the sides of the cake. Alternatively, place the cake on a cake tin to raise its height to a comfortable level.

Spread the icing over the sides of the cake making sure it comes well up to the top edge. Use a scraper with a serrated edge. Position your left hand as far around the cake as possible to hold the turntable or board. Hold the scraper in the right hand at an angle of 45 degrees to the side of the cake. Rotate the cake as the scraper sweeps over the icing in one movement. Release the pressure on the scraper slightly just as you reach the place where you started and quickly pull it away. The point where you pull off the scraper will be the back of the cake. You may have to repeat the process to get a good finish.

PIPING TECHNIQUE AND MORE COMPLICATED DECORATIVE DESIGNS

Develop your cake-decorating skills by following the instructions in this chapter. Lace work, embroidery, run-outs and basket weave icing are all included along with ideas for piping plain or star patterns. Extension work and the knack of making a Garrett frill complete the guidance for the confident cake decorator.

PIPING WITH ROYAL ICING

Fine piping is a skill which is developed with practice; and it calls for a steady hand as well as an artistic approach. Equally important is the quality of the actual icing – if its consistency is wrong, you will never achieve good results. Icing which is too stiff will break the icing bag; if the icing is too slack the design will not hold its shape on the cake.

THE CORRECT CONSISTENCY

The consistency required depends on the type of design which is being piped and the size of the nozzle.

It is better to beat the icing by hand for piping otherwise there may be too many air bubbles in it which might cause the piping to break. Make the icing on the day you intend to use it, otherwise it tends to become heavy. Do leave the icing to stand for a few hours to dispel any air bubbles. Always keep the icing well covered and do not let any particles of dried icing get into the fresh icing. Even the tiniest particles can block a fine nozzle.

THE ICING BAG

Make several paper icing bags (page 18) before you begin, and store them one inside the other. When required, snip off the end of one of the bags and insert the nozzle – put a little icing in the nozzle to weight it if you have difficulty in inserting it. The amount to snip off the bag depends on the nozzle. A writing nozzle needs a small hole of about 5 mm/¼ inch but some larger nozzles, such as petals or shells will need a larger hole. The nozzle should not protrude more than half-way out of the bag, otherwise the paper may split.

Use a teaspoon to fill the icing bag. Fold the top of the icing bag down and hold it between the thumb and forefinger. These fingers will guide the bag, the remaining fingers will provide the pressure. If you are piping without a nozzle, fill the bag before snipping off the point.

PIPING PRACTICE

Choose medium-sized nozzles and practise piping on a tray or work surface until you can regulate the amount of pressure required. Small designs are piped with the minimum of pressure; more pressure is necessary when piping larger designs such as shell or scroll work. It is best to start with a plain writing nozzle size 0 or 1.

CORRECT POSITION

It is important to position the icing bag correctly. For piping on top of the cake it is best to stand up, especially for work where the nozzle is held at an angle of 90 degrees to the cake, for example, when piping stars and beads. When piping on the sides of the cake, sit down and raise the cake on a turntable or cake tin so that it is at eye level.

DESIGNS WITH THE PLAIN WRITING NOZZLE

DOTS OR BEADS

These should resemble small round balls; they must not end in a peak. Place the point of the nozzle on the surface and hold the bag at an angle of 90 degrees to the cake. Start pressing out a little icing – the more you press out, the bigger the dot will be. Do not lift the nozzle away until you have stopped squeezing out the icing otherwise the dot will have a peak.

Small beads can be used to outline or fill in a shape; they can also form part of embroidery work (page 83). Larger beads can be used to edge the top of the cake and the base of the cake can be finished with very large beads. It is important that all the dots are of uniform size.

STRAIGHT LINES

Hold the bag at an angle of 45 degrees to the surface of the cake and support it, if necessary, with the left hand, placed near the nozzle. Place the nozzle on the surface, start squeezing, then raise the nozzle off the surface. Keep squeezing and at the same time slowly move the nozzle towards you so that a thread of icing is formed. Do not pull too quickly or the icing will break; similarly, if you stop squeezing, the icing will break.

Hold the thread of icing about 2.5 cm/1 inch above the surface and let it fall gently into the required position. If you hold the nozzle too near the cake, the line will be crooked. Finish the line by lowering the nozzle and easing off the pressure. Touch the nozzle on to the surface, then quickly lift it off to make a neat end.

PIPING WITH COLOURED ICINGS

First pipe the design in white, then when it is dry, pipe another line directly on top of it in the coloured icing. This will prevent the colour bleeding on to the main surface, especially if a dark colour, such as red, is used.

TRELLIS OR LATTICE WORK

Pipe straight lines parallel to each other then pipe more parallel lines at right angles or aslant. It is important to keep each set of lines parallel.

Dots and Straight Lines

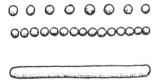

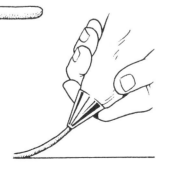

Trellis or Lattice Work

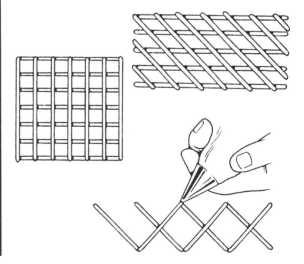

DOUBLE TRELLIS OR LATTICE

Repeat the pattern by piping over the lines of the first set of trellis, in the same order in which they were first piped. Care must be taken when finishing off each line and it is best to extend it just beyond the base trellis and down on to the cake. The trellis can be neatened by piping small beads round the edges.

RAISED LATTICE WORK

This is piped over a shape, such as an upturned bun tin, boat-shaped tartlet mould, or deep-bowled spoon. Lightly grease the mould with lard first. Allow the piping to dry

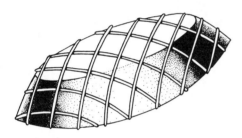

well before carefully lifting it off and arranging it on the cake. Neaten the edges with small piped beads.

FILIGREE, CORNELLI WORK OR SCRIBBLING

Use a no 0 or 1 nozzle; the smaller nozzle gives the most delicate design. The consistency of the icing should be slightly softer

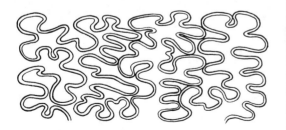

than for straight lines as it should look as though it is part of the flat icing on the cake.

Hold the bag in one hand only and place the nozzle at an angle of 45 degrees to the surface. Start squeezing and moving the bag at random backwards and forwards within a given area, just lifting the nozzle above the surface and occasionally letting it touch the surface. The line should remain unbroken.

When using this technique to fill in an area between a design and the outer edge of a cake, start piping at the edge of the cake and return to the edge before breaking off to rest.

🥣 **MRS BEETON'S TIP** If the top edge of the cake is to be neatened with a shell border, finish the filigree about 3 mm/ ⅛ inch short of the edge. Alternatively, while the icing is still soft, trim the edge with a sharp knife so that there is a flat surface on which to pipe the shell edge.

WRITING

Use a no 1 or 2 nozzle. Writing is better piped freehand than to a pattern. Practise on a tray first so that you know how much space each letter will take.

After the initial letter, pipe lower case letters as these flow more easily and can be piped in a smooth continuous line. Do not attempt to pipe the letters as you would write them, otherwise you will find that you pipe over some lines twice. Form each letter separately, starting at the top and ending with the loop to join it to the next letter. Be careful when removing the nozzle from the letter that you stop squeezing before you lift up the nozzle, otherwise small peaks will make the writing untidy.

Use the same technique as for straight lines but lay the thread of icing down in the curves of the letters. Pipe in white icing, or icing that is the same colour as the surface of the cake. When the piping is dry, pipe over it a second layer of coloured icing if liked, to raise the letters and make them stand out.

EMBROIDERY

This is used on the sides of the cake, instead of ribbon. Occasionally, a few motifs are brought on to the top of the cake in a limited design. For the best effect, the design is piped in a deeper shade or a contrasting colour to the main cake covering, for example white embroidery can be used on a base of blue flat icing.

THE PATTERN

Embroidery is best piped freehand. Tracing or pin-pricking an intricate design produces a mass of confusing holes. Copy lace borders or embroidery transfers and draw the design on a piece of paper cut to the same size as the area which is to be piped. Mark main areas, such as the beginning and end of sections, on the cake. The piping on the cake does not have to be exactly like the pattern and it does not have to be uniform on both sides of the cake.

A variety of simple designs can be used, for example petals, leaves, scrolls, 'S' and 'C' shapes, dots, beads, bows, birds and butterflies. Avoid piping straight lines.

THE ICING AND NOZZLES

Use a soft peak icing (page 41) and check the texture after adding any food colouring. Use a variety of plain writing nozzles to create the texture of the pattern, from no 00 to 0 and 1.

TO PIPE EMBROIDERY

Place the cake on a turntable or cake tin. Sit down to work so that the side of the cake is at eye level.

Hold the nozzle at an angle of 45 degrees to the cake. Use only light pressure, enough to maintain a steady stream of icing as you 'draw' on the cake. Remember to ease off the pressure before you pull away the nozzle, otherwise the icing will peak and the design may well be spoilt.

LACE WORK

Use a no 0 plain writing nozzle. Lace work is made up of small, delicate motifs which are piped on to waxed paper and allowed to dry. They are then lifted off and attached to the cake. The motifs can either be used on their own or with extension work (page 86).

THE PATTERN

Trace your chosen pattern. Use embroidery transfers, a wallpaper pattern or a piece of lace as a guide. Trace the pattern as for run-outs (page 88). You will need to pipe about twice as many patterns as you will need to allow for breakages. Trace the pattern ten or twelve times on card and move this along under the waxed paper as you complete the motifs.

THE ICING

This should be of a thinner consistency than for ordinary piping as it must flow smoothly through a fine hole and the joins should flow together as one. However, the icing must be thick enough to hold a good, clear shape.

TO PIPE THE LACE

Hold the nozzle at an angle of 45 degrees, using only sufficient pressure to enable a thin stream of icing to flow. Hold the nozzle close to the paper for greater control. Take care when joining icing to make sure the join is neat and free of any ugly peaks. Use a pin to move the edge of the icing, if necessary. Ensure that all loops are connected, otherwise they will be left behind when the lace is removed from the paper.

ATTACHING THE LACE TO THE CAKE

Leave the lace to dry for at least 24 hours. Use a palette knife or round-ended knife to lift the lace off the paper, moving it gently on the paper first. Pipe small dots or a thin line on to the cake where the lace is to be attached. Carefully hold the motif in position for a second on the wet icing to ensure that it is secure. The lace should be at an angle of 45 degrees to the surface of the cake. Even the most experienced cake decorator will have some breakages, so make sure that you have plenty of motifs at the ready. Any remaining motifs can be stored between layers of greaseproof paper in a box for future use.

Alternatively, instead of piping the wet icing on to the surface of the cake, it can be piped on to the lace, then pressed on to the cake as part of the motif.

MRS BEETON'S TIP When fine nozzles are used the icing tends to dry on the tip. Keep a clean, damp cloth handy and wipe the end of the nozzle occasionally to keep it clean and to keep the icing in the bag damp and free flowing.

Designs for Lace Work

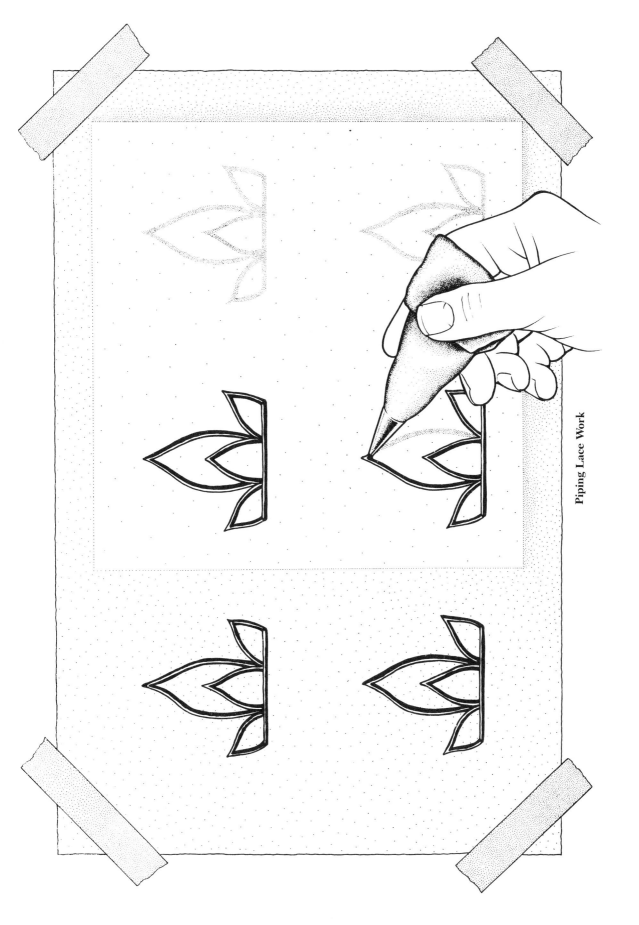

Piping Lace Work

EXTENSION WORK

This delicate piping is used round the side of the cake, near the base, and it stands out from the side of the cake. Allow plenty of time for each layer to dry before adding the next. All these designs require patience and skill, and plenty of time. Extension work is made up of bridge work – built up layers of plain piping in the shape required, usually scalloped – and curtain work. Curtain work is fine parallel lines of icing placed close together. The bottom edge of the design is often scalloped but the top edge may be scalloped or straight. The work is usually about 2.5 cm/1 inch in length and very close together. Extension work can either be brought down almost on to the board, or it can be finished above a row of shells or stars around the base of the cake. These decorations are piped on the cake when all the other icing is complete. Once the work is finished the cake must be handled with extreme care to prevent any breakages from occurring.

THE ICING AND NOZZLES

Two nozzles are used: no 2 for bridge work and a finer nozzle for curtains. Start with size 0 but progress to 00 and eventually 000 when you have mastered the technique.

Use a soft peak icing for the bridge work and a softer peak for the curtain work. Keep the nozzle clean while piping.

THE PATTERN

Cut a paper pattern to exactly fit the sides of the cake. Fold the paper, cut scallop shapes and mark them on to the cake by pricking or scratching the icing with a pin.

Mark a second pattern of scallops or a straight line pattern on the cake 2.5 cm/1 inch above the first marks.

PIPING EXTENSION WORK

Scallops or Bridge work Start with the larger nozzle (no 1 or 2) and pipe a thick line around the base of the cake where it joins the board. Alternatively, pipe a row of stars or shells here.

1 Pipe a row of shells around the base of the cake.

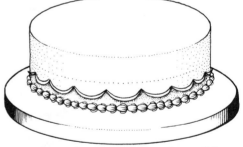

2 Mark out the top and bottom lines of the extension work and pipe the scallops.

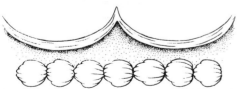

3 The scallops are built up with several lines of icing: this is known as bridge work.

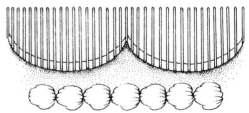

4 Fine threads of icing are piped from the line which marks the top of the extension work to the top of the scallops, or bridge work. This is known as the curtain.

Use a large plain nozzle and pipe the scallops by placing the nozzle on to the cake at the beginning of one scallop. Press out the icing and lift the nozzle, then move it along close to the cake so that a fine line of icing can be laid in position on the marked scallop. Ensure that the icing touches the cake all along the scallop otherwise it will weaken the next stage of the extension work. Continue piping all the scallops around the cake, then leave the icing to dry at least 15 minutes before piping a second line of icing on top of the first one. Continue to build up the scallops until the icing is five or six layers deep. Leave to dry overnight.

The Curtains Using the fine nozzle, start by placing a tiny blob of icing on the line marked above the scallops. Push out a fine thread of icing as you lift the nozzle and draw it downwards and outwards towards the bridgework on the scallop shape below. Tuck the end of the icing in just under the bridgework. Use a pin or fine paint brush to help, if necessary.

Continue piping these threads parallel to each other from the top line, down to the scallop shape. They should be so close together that there is no room for a thread between them. This work takes some time to complete and it should be piped in sections, starting with a fresh bag of icing and clean nozzle each time.

FINISHING THE EXTENSION WORK

Leave the work to dry overnight before neatening the edges with a row of small beads. Lace motifs can be added to create an elaborate finish along the top line.

TIPS FOR SUCCESS WITH DELICATE PIPING

■ When piping a lace design or any other very small motifs, always make many more than required to allow for breakages.

■ When piping delicate designs, always check that the icing is of the right consistency and practice piping one motif or shape so that you get the 'feel' of the icing before you start.

■ Always have a strong, well-made icing bag. If the bag feels as though it is about to break, then start afresh with a new bag and icing rather than ruin the icing.

■ Always leave delicate pieces of piped icing to dry thoroughly before attempting to remove them from the card. When piping extension work, always leave the layers of piping to dry thoroughly as directed.

■ When piping extension work on a cake, make sure that you have decided on the complete pattern for the decoration on the cake. Mark it clearly and accurately on the cake before you start.

■ Allow plenty of time for piping these delicate designs and make sure that you are standing or sitting in a comfortable position before you start.

■ Take great care when moving the finished cake as lace work and extension work are particularly delicate.

RUN-OUTS

Royal icing sets very hard and it can be used for quite delicate decorations, collars and plaques. A run-out consists of a shape which is piped on to waxed paper, then flooded with a softer icing and allowed to set. When hard, the shape is strong enough to lift off the paper and transfer to its position on the cake. Run-outs can be used on the sides of the cake where piping is difficult.

The run-out can be made in any shape – a club emblem, badge, numbers, letters and/or characters. They can be made in white icing and painted with food colouring when dry. Alternatively, the icing can be coloured first if not too many colours are required. Allow plenty of time to pipe the run-outs and let them dry thoroughly, preferably for up to a week. Make several as they are fragile and may break when handled.

THE DESIGNS

Choose simple designs that can be piped in sections. Trace shapes from Christmas and birthday cards, wrapping paper, gift tags, children's books and posters.

THE ICING AND NOZZLE

Outlines are piped with a no 1 plain writing nozzle. A well-made paper icing bag is required for the flooding. The icing should be of a soft peak consistency for the outlines. Add a little lemon juice or water to make a softer consistency for the flooding. For flooding, the consistency should be that of thick cream that slowly finds its own level; if the icing is too slack the run-outs will be thin and very fragile. Icing made with egg white gives a smoother surface than icing made with albumen. Designs that have several different colours are best piped in white and painted over when dry. This gives a stronger colour and is useful for figure run-outs such as Father Christmas. For less complicated designs, colour the icing first, remembering that only a tiny dot of colour is required.

Use a sharp, dark pencil to trace the design on to a piece of greaseproof paper. Reverse the paper and trace over the outline again. Turn the paper over and lay it on a piece of thin white card. Trace over the design once more and a faint mark will be transferred on to the card. Trace the design three or four more times over different parts of the card, then go over the images carefully so that they are quite clear.

Attach the card to a firm, flat, portable surface such as a large chopping board, upturned tray or large cake board. Use tape or drawing pins to keep the card firmly in place. Cover with a piece of waxed paper or non-stick baking parchment and secure it perfectly flat with tape or drawing pins at the corners. If the paper is crumpled or creased the run-outs will not dry flat.

PIPING RUN-OUTS

The designs are piped in sections, allowing each one to dry briefly before piping the next section. This creates run-outs of height; otherwise they would be flat and uninteresting. Divide the design into sections and start with sections that do not touch each other.

Using soft peak icing, hold the nozzle at an angle of 45 degrees to the paper at a suitable starting point on the design. Press out a thread of icing as you lift the nozzle, then lay the icing down on the pattern. Pipe all around the outline of one section, leaving no gaps.

Fill a strong paper icing bag with softer icing; snip off the end to make a small hole. Flood the outlined area by moving the bag backwards and forwards as the icing flows out. Keep the point of the bag under the icing until the area is covered and slightly domed. Use a pin or skewer to tease the icing into difficult corners. Tap the board gently on the table or run a palette knife quickly from side to side under the waxed paper if you have difficulty in making the icing flow.

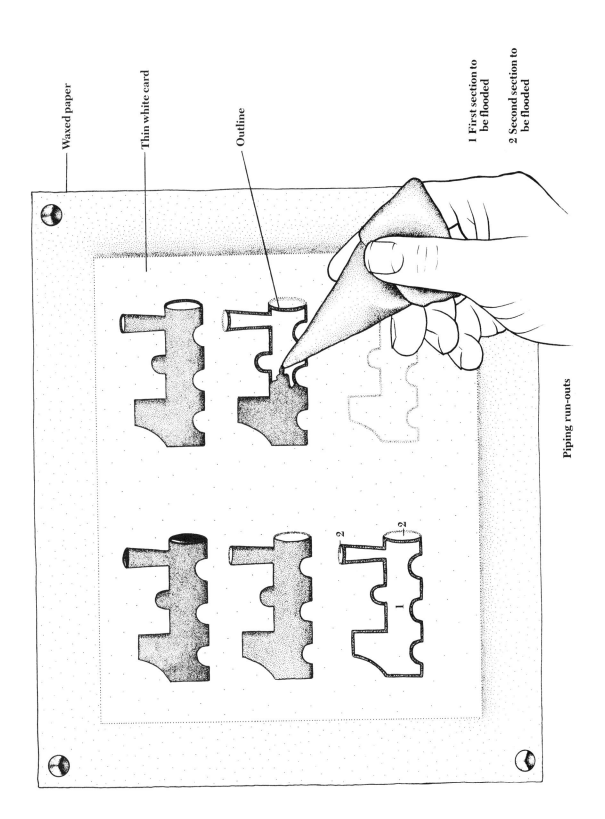

Waxed paper

Thin white card

Outline

1 First section to be flooded

2 Second section to be flooded

Piping run-outs

If any air bubbles appear, prick them with a pin.

The flooding should slightly bevel-out on to the outline to hide it but it should not flow over it. The exception is when the outline has been piped in a contrasting colour to give form to the design, for example, the shape of an arm which might otherwise be difficult to define. Fill the outline as full as possible as the icing tends to shrink on drying. Leave each section for about 20 minutes or more, before outlining and flooding the adjacent section.

For a shiny surface, the icing must be dried as quickly as possible. Place the run-out under a table lamp, if possible, for 10 minutes before placing it in a warm, dry atmosphere. An airing cupboard is ideal; the icing will not dry in a damp place.

TO REMOVE RUN-OUTS FROM THE PAPER

If several run-outs have been worked on one sheet of paper, it is a good idea to cut around each of them with a razor blade leaving a large margin of paper all around. With care, the paper can be peeled away from each run-out. Alternatively, use a palette knife to ease between the icing and the paper. Handle run-outs carefully – remember that some designs will have weak areas.

ATTACHING RUN-OUTS TO THE CAKE

Pipe a little royal icing on to the underside of the run-out and attach it to the cake. Do not press hard on the run-out once placed in position or it may crack.

SMALL DESIGNS

An alternative method to use for small run-outs is to use the same icing and nozzle for both the outline and the flooding. Make the outline in the same way, then fill the centre by pressing the icing out and moving the nozzle at an angle of 45 degrees very slowly in small circular movements. This method is only suitable for small designs as it takes a long time to fill and smooth the flooding.

MRS BEETON'S TIP When you have mastered the technique of making run-outs, a one-off design can be run-out directly on to the surface of the cake.

TIPS FOR SUCCESS WITH RUNOUTS

■ Select a design that has distinct areas which can be flooded with icing. Do not attempt too intricate a design if you are a beginner.

■ Make sure that the pattern is clearly drawn and visible through the paper before you begin.

■ Make sure that both the pattern and the paper cover are secured to the board. Use pins or masking tape. Clear sticky tape does not come away easily and in trying to remove it you may break the run-out.

■ Decide which areas are to be flooded at the same time. Do not try to flood neighbouring sections that may flow together.

■ When one area of the run-out is flooded, leave it to dry completely before flooding a neighbouring area.

■ Make sure that the run-out is thoroughly dried before removing it from the paper.

DESIGNS USING STAR AND SHELL NOZZLES

The star nozzle is particularly versatile, as it can be used for piping stars, scrolls, ropes and shells and it makes a more delicate design than the shell nozzle which is thicker and uses a lot of icing. These nozzles are available in various sizes but the medium and small sizes are easier to use. The final size of the design will, however, be determined by the amount of pressure used when piping.

The icing should have the consistency of a medium peak (page 41). Practise on the table or a board first to determine the size of your design, especially if you are using coloured icing which tends to mark a base coat of white icing.

USING THE STAR NOZZLE

Stars Work directly over the cake, holding the icing bag at an angle of 90 degrees to the surface. Hold the end of the bag in closed fingers and try to use one hand only for piping the stars. Holding the nozzle just off the cake, squeeze the bag gently, then stop pressing before you lift up the nozzle. If you remove the nozzle while still pressing the star will end in a peak. For bigger stars, press out more icing before removing the bag. Pipe the stars so that they are just touching each other. For an elaborate star border, using a writing nozzle, loop a fine thread of plain icing from the top of one star to the next.

Scrolls Hold the nozzle as for a star but maintain the pressure and twist the nozzle in an 'S' shape. Then release the pressure and pull the nozzle away quickly to make a thin tail. The scrolls can be joined up to form a continuous edging or they can be piped in alternate directions for a more decorative finish.

Rope Borders Keeping an even pressure on the bag and holding the nozzle at an angle of 45 degrees to the cake, press out a thick line of royal icing using a circular movement to form a cable or rope.

USING THE SHELL NOZZLE

Shells Hold the nozzle at an angle of 45 degrees to the cake and squeeze out a rounded shape, lifting the nozzle slightly and replacing it again in the same place, then releasing the pressure and pulling the nozzle away along the cake to form a tail. Start the next shell at the end of the preceding tail so that the rounded shell shape slightly overlaps the tail. Use the tip of a pointed knife to tuck the last tail into position if necessary.

Star

Rope

Scroll

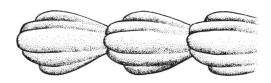

Shells

Basket Weave Icing

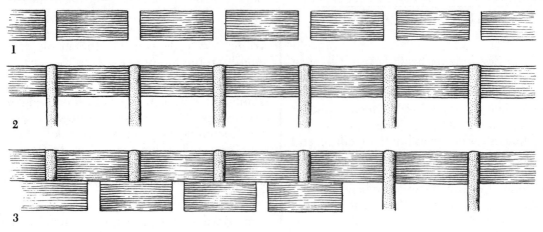

Alternative Method

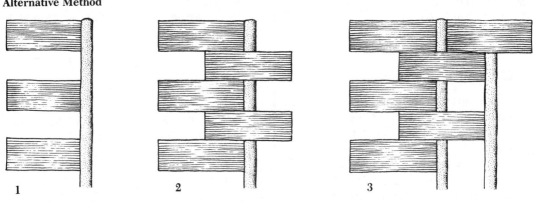

BASKET WEAVE ICING

This design can be piped in buttercream over a sponge cake, but the royal icing gives a neater effect. Allow plenty of time to pipe this design. The icing should be of a medium-peak consistency. For the best effect, use coloured icing. You will need a plain writing nozzle no 2 for the vertical lines and a basket or serrated ribbon nozzle for the horizontal piping. Have both nozzles fitted in separate bags of icing ready before you begin.

The design is often piped on the sides of the cake, so raise the cake so that it is at eye level by placing it on a turntable or cake tin.

Sit down for steady, controlled piping.

Start at the back of the cake with the serrated nozzle and pipe a 2.5 cm/1 inch long ribbon horizontally around the cake at the top edge. Leave a gap the same width as the ribbon and pipe another ribbon horizontally underneath the first, beginning and ending at the same place as the first. Repeat these parallel lines of piping, leaving a gap between each one until you reach the base of the cake.

Using the icing bag fitted with the plain nozzle, pipe a vertical line down the cake at the point where the ribbons end.

Using the serrated nozzle, pipe a second row of 2.5 cm/1 inch long ribbons over the vertical line and in between the first line of ribbons. Begin piping each ribbon parallel to the ribbon above and halfway along it. Now pipe another vertical line with the plain nozzle. Continue in this way all around the cake to build up the pattern. Finish the bottom and top edge of the cake with a shell border (page 91).

ALTERNATIVE METHOD

Alternatively, using exactly the same technique, the basket weave icing can be worked in horizontal rows. To do this pipe a line of 2.5 cm/1 inch ribbons, with a space between each, all around the cake. Next pipe the vertical, straight lines, then pipe another horizontal row of ribbons underneath. Continue building up the pattern in this way.

GARRETT FRILL

This is the frilled edge of a strip of sugar paste which is used to edge iced cakes or for making moulded flowers.

The sugar paste must be rolled out paper thin – a laminex board and rolling pin are very useful for this purpose to prevent the paste from sticking to the surface. Cover any paste which is not being used. Use only a very fine dusting of cornflour when rolling the paste, otherwise the paste will become dry and break easily. The edge of the rolled paste is stretched into a frill, using a cocktail stick or a wooden dowel.

PREPARING THE CAKE

Make a paper pattern to fit halfway around the sides of the cake. Fold the paper 2 or 3 times then mark and cut out a shallow curve. Open out the paper, transfer it to thin card and use a pin to scratch the design around the cake, about 2.5 cm/1 inch up from the base at the lowest point of the curve. Pipe a

row of stars or shells around the lower edge of the cake or use a thin roll of paste to neaten the edge.

MAKING THE FRILL

Method 1 Roll out a small piece of paste, paper thin, and trim it to a strip measuring 2.5 cm/1 inch wide and 10 cm/4 inches long.

Lay a cocktail stick flat on the board, overlapping the sugar paste by about 1 cm/½ inch. Place your index finger on the stick at the edge of the paste, then firmly and quickly roll the stick backwards and forwards until the paste frills. Move the stick along the edge and continue until the whole strip is frilled. Dust the cocktail stick with a little cornflour occasionally.

Quickly brush the marked line on the cake with a damp brush – this is where the frill is to be attached. Place the unfrilled edge of the strip of paste on to the cake, holding it for a few seconds until it sticks. Gently lift up the edge of the frill with the blunt end of the brush. Repeat this process, all round the cake, overlapping the frill a little at each join.

Method 2 Use a 7.5 cm/3 inch Garrett frill cutter, or fluted cutter, to cut out thin circles of paste. Stamp out their centres with a 3.5 cm/1½ inch plain cutter.

Frill the edges of the rings of paste as in the previous method. Cut the ring and open it out. Alternatively, cut the ring in half to make smaller curves. Attach the frill as in the first method.

A second layer of frills can be attached to the cake once the first one is dry. To neaten the top edge of the frill, either prick it decoratively with a cocktail stick or pipe a row of small beads along it.

> **MRS BEETON'S TIP** To strengthen the frill, knead a small piece of petal paste (pages 13 and 94) into the sugar paste before you begin.

MAKING MOULDED AND PIPED DECORATIONS

A variety of decorations can be made at home and, with practice, they can be far superior to the shop-bought alternatives. As well as moulded and piped flowers for formal cakes, this chapter shows how to make run-outs and colourful marzipan fruits or vegetables.

The choice of decorations that are added to a plain iced cake will depend on the type of icing used for covering the cake, as it is much easier to use the same icing rather than making up a totally different type. However, for very special occasions, when the decorations are made well in advance or even stored for future use, it is worth taking the trouble to create an elaborately designed cake which may be decorated with piped royal icing on a base of a softer, moulded icing.

One important factor to keep in mind is your own ability. Plan to make decorations which you are confident will turn out well. If this is your first or second attempt at cake decorating, it is safer and more sensible to follow some of the simpler techniques.

Within this chapter you will find instructions for making a variety of decorations, some easier than others. Allow yourself plenty of time and make more decorations than you need to finish the cake and you are unlikely to have a disaster. Indeed, you may be surprised at how successful you are.

MOULDING PASTES

A variety of decorations can be moulded using marzipan, sugar paste or petal paste.

WHITE MARZIPAN

This is smoother than almond paste and will absorb colours more readily. It is suitable for making figures, vegetables, fruits, leaves and larger flowers such as roses. The marzipan will dry if left in a dry, warm atmosphere but it will remain soft enough to eat. Use icing sugar for rolling it out and for moulding the pieces.

PETAL PASTE

This is a paste which is made specifically for modelling flowers and similar decorations. The paste sets hard and it is quite strong once it has set. However the decorations are usually too hard to eat. Use cornflour for rolling out and modelling.

SUGAR PASTE OR MOULDING ICING

These are easy to use and they dry hard but they are not as strong as petal paste. For a good compromise, knead a small piece of made-up petal paste (about the size of a walnut) into 225 g/8 oz sugar paste. Use cornflour for rolling out and modelling.

MATCHING COLOURS

When colouring the marzipan or paste remember to keep small balls of the coloured paste for matching up with any batches that may have to be made later. Keep the pieces of coloured paste wrapped in cling film inside a plastic bag or jar.

MRS BEETON'S TIP To avoid using too much cornflour when handling the paste, use a new, clean powder puff to dust the surface, rolling pin and hands with cornflour.

MOULDED LEAVES

There are several methods of making leaves; the following are all suitable for marzipan, petal paste or moulding icing.

Method 1 Roll out the paste thickly and use a leaf cutter to stamp out the leaves. Carefully peel away excess paste, then lift the leaves off with a palette knife and spread them out on non-stick baking parchment until dry.

Method 2 Roll out the paste thickly and cut it into diamond-shaped pieces of the required size. Either smooth the edges to form leaves or cut out small pieces around the leaf using a tiny plain cutter or the wide end of an icing nozzle.

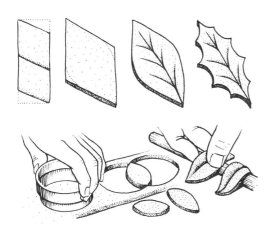

Method 3 Using a round plain cutter, stamp out a circle. Place the cutter three quarters of the way across the circle and cut again to give an oval-shaped leaf.

TO FINISH·THE LEAVES

Use a small pointed knife to mark the veins on the leaves. Dry some of the leaves over a small rolling pin, empty foil roll or pencil so that they curve. Alternatively, place the leaves in a box lined with crumpled foil so that they dry into uneven shapes.

MOULDED FLOWERS

Roses and daisies are the easiest flowers to mould, but once you have mastered the techniques you will be able to create a variety of different flowers. Study real flowers (or use seed catalogues or other pictures as reference) for guidance. If you have real flowers to copy keep one in water just beside you. Carefully pull another one apart to study the shape of the petals and the way in which they are assembled. Small posies or miniature baskets of flowers can be made from Petal Paste (pages 13 and 94). The paste gives the moulded shapes strength; once dry they will keep indefinitely for permanent display. Shaped cutters are available for stamping out simple petal shapes but those that are moulded free-hand look more authentic.

The flowers can be made in white paste and painted with food colouring when dry or they can be moulded in a coloured paste in which case they should be tinted with extra colour when dry to make each flower individual. Marzipan is only suitable for the larger flowers such as roses, as it cannot be moulded as thinly as the other pastes.

DRYING THE FLOWERS

The flowers need to be supported as they dry – they can be placed on trays lined with non-stick baking parchment, in boxes lined with crumpled foil or rested in the holes of a wire cake cooling rack.

POINSETTIA

Using a deeply tinted red-coloured paste, cut large diamond leaf shapes from rolled out paste and leave them to dry over a rolling pin. Arrange the dried petals in a circle each slightly overlapping its neighbour. Make the stamen with piped icing or use small sugar cake decorations. Leave to dry on crumpled greaseproof paper.

SMALL DAISY

Take a small ball of white paste and shape it into a cone. Pinch the thin end into a stalk and ease out the other end with the fingertips (or use a modelling tool with a ball end) until it is thin and shaped like a shallow

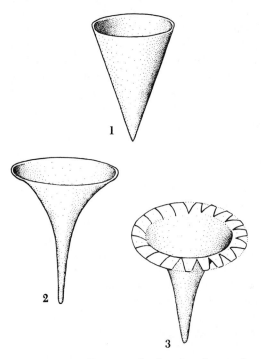

bowl. Snip all around the bowl at short intervals with scissors to make the petals. Prick the middle of the daisy to make the centre and leave to dry on crumpled paper. To finish, paint the centre yellow and tip some of the petals with pink.

LARGE DAISY

Make as for the small daisy but use a larger ball of paste and after cutting ten petals, snip each petal to a point with the scissors and curl them outwards to dry. Instead of pricking the centre for the stamen, mould a small ball of yellow paste, prick it with scissors and stick it into the centre of the

daisy by brushing the base with a dampened paint brush.

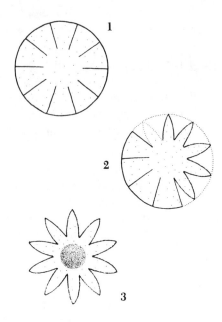

DOUBLE DAISY

Make two sets of petals as for the large daisy,

one slightly smaller than the other. Stick the smaller one inside the larger. Finish as for the large daisy.

AFRICAN VIOLET

Using violet-coloured paste, form a long thin cone and mould a large hole in the thicker

end with the blunt end of a pen or paint brush. Snip around to make fine petals and gently flatten and ease the petals outwards. Trim off the sharp corners of each petal, then mould each one into a very thin round-shaped petal. The petals should be almost spread out flat. Stick tiny balls of deep yellow paste in the centre for stamens.

ROSE

Mould a piece of paste the size of a pea into a cone and stand it pointing upwards on the table. Take another piece of paste the same size and hold it in the left hand. With the

right thumb on top of the paste and the other fingers underneath, mould and pull the paste outwards into a very thin petal. Wrap the narrow end of the petal around the base of the cone. The tighter it is wrapped, the tighter the resulting bud.

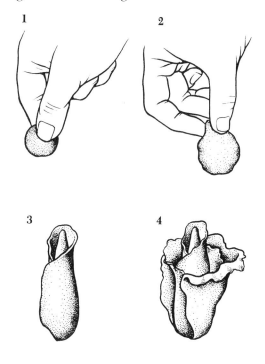

Repeat the process, making and wrapping more petals, each one slightly larger than the preceding one and wrapped more loosely around the bud. Gently roll the edge of the petals outwards. Vary the number of petals used to make flowers of different sizes, from buds through to fully opened specimens. Do not add too many petals or the shape will resemble a tightly packed cabbage rather than a loosely open rose! Trim the base off the rose to a slant and leave it to dry, supported on a tray or on crumpled foil.

It is best to make one rose at a time so that the petals readily stick to each other. If preferred, several roses can be shaped at once, in which case brush the base of each rose with a damp paint brush before mould-ing on a new petal.

CARNATION

The technique for making a carnation is the same as for making a Garret frill (page 93), where the edge of the paste is frilled with a wooden cocktail stick. Strengthen the moulding icing with a piece of petal paste.

The paste (marzipan is not suitable for this) is rolled paper-thin preferably using a laminex board and rolling pin.

The rolled-out paste is cut with a special carnation cutter or a small fluted pastry cutter about 4 cm/1½ inches in diameter. The carnation is built up from four circles. These can all be cut out together but remember to place cling film over any circles not being moulded.

Lightly dust a board with cornflour and roll out the paste as thinly as paper, picking it up and rotating it around as you roll it to prevent it from sticking. Cut out four circles, peel away excess paste and cover three of the circles with cling film.

With the pointed end of a knife, cut 5 mm/ ¼ inch slits at frequent intervals all around the remaining circle. Lay a cocktail stick flat on the surface with one pointed end overlapping the circle of paste between two slits. Use your index finger to roll the stick backwards and forwards until the edge of the paste frills and flutes between the slits. Frill the edge between all the slits in the same way, dusting the stick with cornflour, as necessary.

Fold the fluted circle into four and pinch the base together. Frill and fold two of the remaining circles in the same way. Flute the remaining circle but do not fold it. Pinch the three folded circles together and place them in the centre of the flat circle. Pinch the bases together. Brush the bases with a damp paint brush, if necessary, to ensure that they stick in the fourth circle to make the completed carnation. Leave the carnation to dry, supported in a wire rack.

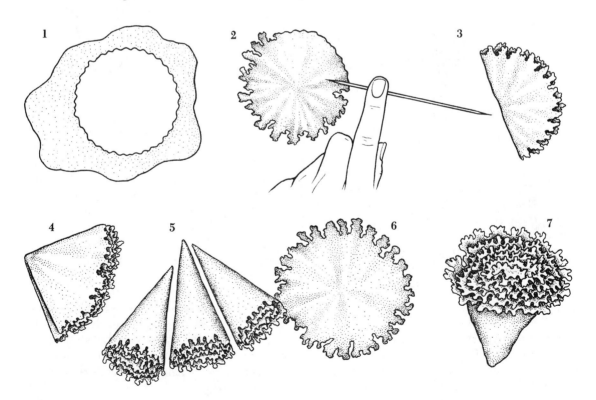

Shaping Daffodils

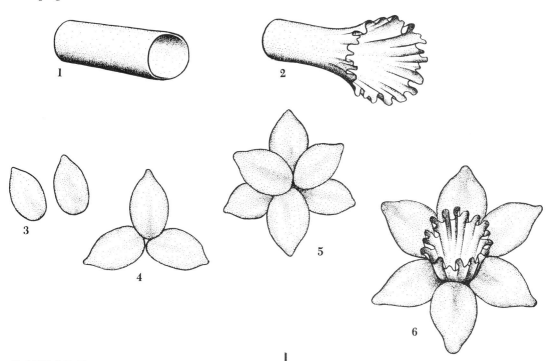

DAFFODIL

Daffodils can be made with marzipan or petal paste. Do not make them too large or they will flop or dwarf your other flowers. Allow several days for the flowers to dry. The daffodils are laid on the cake and the stalks added when they are in position.

Start each daffodil by shaping the trumpet: mould a small roll, about 2 cm/¾ inch long, from bright yellow paste. Insert the blunt end of a clean pencil into one end to make the hollow trumpet. Open out the end and thin the paste out with the fingers, then frill it with a cocktail stick (as for making a carnation, page 98). Cut a thin slice off the blunt end, then leave the trumpet to dry.

While the trumpet is drying, make the petals. If using marzipan, mould by hand to six petal shapes about 2.5 cm/1 inch long. They should be wider at the base than the tip. If using petal paste, roll it out thinly and cut out petal shapes. Arrange three petals, bases overlapping, to form a triangle, then place the other three on top, in between the first three. Lightly pinch the tips of the petals to soften the edge. Mould the petals over a crumpled ball of foil with the tips just touching the work surface so that they curl outwards. Pinch the centre of the petals together, gently moulding the paste into a small knob; this will be the position for the stalk. Leave to dry for 24 hours. Stick the trumpet inside the petals and lay the daffodil on crumpled foil.

To make the stamens, roll a tiny piece of white paste into a very thin roll and cut it into 2.5 cm/1 inch lengths. Place several together and put them into the trumpet. Add small blobs of yellow paste for tips, or pipe these in royal icing. Finish the daffodil by moulding two thin green leaves; wrapping them round the base of the flower, squeezing their ends together and bending them at right angles to the flower to form the beginning of the stalk. Arrange the dried daffodils on the cake and add rolls of green paste to represent stalks.

MOULDED FIGURES AND ANIMALS

These can be made with sugar paste or marzipan. The finished figures should be left to dry for up to seven days in a dry place. Protect them from dust by draping them loosely with greaseproof paper, allowing air to circulate around them.

SNOWMAN

If making several, knead colour into a small piece of paste; black for hats, eyes and buttons; a small orange piece for noses and a small red piece for scarves. Alternatively, if only making one or two, make the figure all in white and paint the colour on the features after twenty-four hours.

You will need 40 g/1½ oz marzipan or paste for each snowman, allowing 25 g/1 oz to mould into the body. Cut the remaining piece in half. Use one piece for the head, taking off a tiny piece to mould into a carrot-shaped nose.

Divide the final piece into three: use one piece to mould arms, one piece to mould into a floppy hat and roll the last piece into a thin sausage. Slightly flatten the sausage to make a scarf and cut both ends with scissors or a knife to make a fringe.

Assembling the Snowman Coat the body, head and arms in icing sugar. Arrange the body and arms in position, dampening them with a paint brush dipped in boiled water or alcohol. Attach the nose, scarf and hat.

DUCK

Use 25 g/1 oz of yellow marzipan or paste for each duck and mould three-quarters of it into a large tear-drop shape for the body.

Flick up the thin end to make the tail. Cut a tiny piece of paste from the remaining piece to make a beak. Flatten it out and cut it into a small diamond shape measuring not more than 5 mm/¼ inch at the widest point. Use the remaining paste to make a ball for the head and place it in position. Bend the beak in half, then insert it into position using the blunt end of a paint brush to push the middle of the beak into the head. Using scissors, cut a 'V' shaped slit on either side of the body to represent wings. Using white royal icing in an icing bag fitted with a plain writing nozzle, pipe beads for eyes or add tiny balls of paste. Leave to dry for 24 hours, then paint the beak bright yellow.

MARZIPAN FRUITS AND VEGETABLES

White marzipan is better than almond paste for moulding these fruits and vegetables because it is smoother and more pliable. It is also more suitable for tinting with food colouring. Study the real fruit or vegetable, or have it in front of you, to achieve the best result. Use icing sugar to dust your fingers while you work. Colour one small piece of marzipan yellow and another green as the two basic colours. To do this, knead the food colouring into the marzipan. Small pieces of these colours can be moulded into the remaining marzipan as required. Most fruits and vegetables are painted for optimum effect; this should be done 24 hours after shaping, when the marzipan has dried slightly.

Use cloves to represent the calyx and stalk on fruit. The fine side of a grater is used to simulate the rough skin of citrus fruits. Mould leaves out of marzipan. The fruit can also be half dipped in chocolate (page 115) or rolled in caster sugar. The marzipan can be moulded around a shelled hazelnut or raisin.

The finished fruits and vegetables may be used to decorate large or small cakes. They may also be packed in paper sweet cases and presented as a charming home-made gift.

FRUIT

Lemon Roll into a ball and ease out to a soft point at each end. Roll lightly on a fine grater.

Apple Roll into a ball, indent top and use a clove for the stalk. Streak with red food colouring.

Pear Gradually taper a ball into shape and put a clove in the narrow end for a stalk. Add another clove to the rounded end for a calyx. Streak with green food colouring.

Banana Shape into a curved sausage, tapering either end. Colour the tip brown and streak the middle with brown 'ripening' lines using a brown icing pen or food colouring, lightly applied with a brush.

Orange Use orange-coloured marzipan. Mould into a ball and roll on a fine grater.

Strawberry Shape into a ball then pinch out one end. Paint with red food colouring and sprinkle with caster sugar at once.

Cherries Shape small balls of red marzipan and add long marzipan stalks. These are the ideal shape in which to conceal a hazelnut or raisin.

Peaches Roll into a ball and indent the top, flattening the paste slightly. Brush with a hint of red food colouring.

VEGETABLES

Parsnips and Carrots Roll into a long cone shape. Mark ridges with a knife or paint these on using thin wisps of brown food colouring. Use orange marzipan for the carrot.

Baby Turnips Use white marzipan. Start with a ball and slightly flatten the top. Paint the top with streaks of purple food colouring and add marzipan leaves.

Mushrooms Cut out a small circle from pink marzipan, and a large piece of white marzipan. Cup the white over the pink, then mark the pink to represent the underside of a mushroom. Add a stalk.

Cauliflower Press lots of small balls of white marzipan together to represent the florets. Mould leaves from green marzipan and press them around the florets.

Peas Mould small green balls. Mould a thin, open pod and put the green balls in it.

Cabbages Make as for moulded roses (page 97), using green marzipan.

PIPED DECORATIONS

These are made with royal icing and are piped on to waxed paper. When dry they are quite brittle. They can be painted, tinted or sprinkled with lustre powder. They keep well for many months when stored between layers of greaseproof paper in a box. Always make many more than you need.

Success depends mainly on having the icing at the correct consistency. This should be firm peak and stiff enough to hold a clean, thin shape once piped. However, it must not be so stiff that your arm aches as you pipe or the icing bag bursts. Flowers are piped on to a special flower nail; you can make one of these by sticking a cork on to a short knitting needle. Some flowers, such as roses, are easier to make when piped around a cocktail stick.

PIPED ROSES

Nozzles Petal nozzles come in a variety of sizes but the smaller sizes are easier to use. The nozzle has a thin end which forms the top of the petal and a bulbous end for the petal base. Take care not to distort the thin end of the nozzle or let it get blocked with icing as this will spoil the piped edge of the petals. If you are left-handed, use an appropriate petal nozzle and reverse all the piping instructions.

Piping the roses This is a time-consuming task, so seat yourself at a comfortable height with the work surface – about elbow height is best. Have ready several cocktail sticks and a supply of waxed paper squares, about 2.5 x 2.5 cm/1 x 1 inch. Place two or three tablespoons of icing into a paper icing bag (page 18) fitted with a petal nozzle. Fold over the top of the bag so that when the top of the bag is held under the fingers, the thin part of the nozzle points upwards. Pierce a square of waxed paper on a cocktail stick positioning this half way down; the paper is used to remove the rose after it has been piped. Hold the stick in your left hand and pipe a strip of icing around the tip, rotating the stick anti-clockwise as you pipe. This forms the central bud.

Hold the nozzle at an angle of 45 degrees to the bud and start at the base of the bud. Squeeze out the icing, lifting up the nozzle and returning it almost immediately to the base of the bud about one-third of the way around. Rotate the stick slowly with the left hand so that the right hand moves up and down, *not* around.

Make two more petals around the bud, slightly overlapping each one at the base. Remember to lift the nozzle for a rounded edge to the petals. Add two or three slightly larger petals around the outside. Do not add too many petals or the rose will resemble a cabbage. Make rosebuds as well as blooms.

Tease the petals gently outwards with a dry paint brush, then slide the paper up the

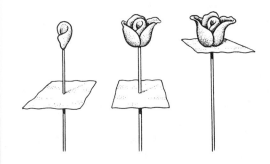

stick until it rests under the rose. Support the base of the rose with your thumb and push the paper off the stick. Make more roses in the same way, then leave the roses to dry for 48 hours. When dried, the roses can be painted and brushed with lustre, if you like.

Two-tone or Tinted Roses These can be made by placing a stream of icing in a contrasting colour down the inside edge of the icing bag when it is filled. Put this icing on the same side as the narrow end of the nozzle. As you pipe, the tips of the petals will be tinted with contrasting icing.

PIPED BLOSSOM

Fit the same nozzle as for piping roses but use a flower nail instead of a cocktail stick. Stick a piece of waxed paper on to the nail with a little icing. Hold the bag horizontally above the nail, with the bulbous end towards the centre. Slowly rotate the nail, squeeze the bag and pipe a petal that covers a quarter of a circle like a fan. Stop squeezing, lift the nozzle and pipe another four petals in the same way. Overlap the petals at the centre base until they are piped in a complete circle. Carefully remove the paper from the nail and leave the flower to dry for a few hours. Fill a paper icing bag fitted with a writing nozzle with yellow icing and pipe small yellow blobs in the centre for stamens.

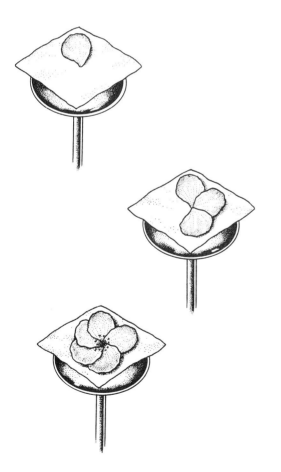

PIPED LEAVES

Long feathery leaves can be piped directly on to the cake or on to a sheet of waxed paper or non-stick baking parchment.

Nozzles Special nozzles that resemble an inverted 'V' can be purchased. For piping a few leaves, the end of a paper icing bag can be cut to a 'V' shape. Renew the bag if the leaves begin to lose their definition.

Piping the Leaves Make a paper icing bag with a good point (page 18). Snip off either side of the point of the bag to make an inverted 'V' shape. The cuts should be between 3-5 mm/⅛-¼ inch in length from the tip to the side of the bag. The tip of the 'V' marks the vein in the leaf.

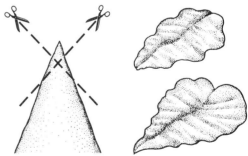

Place two tablespoons of green icing in the bag, fold down the end and hold it in the right hand with the point at an angle of 45 degrees to the paper. The index finger of the left hand can be used to steady the bag and to give slight pressure near the base of the bag, if necessary. Squeeze out the icing, then ease off the pressure and pull the bag away to draw the icing into a point. For a fuller leaf, quickly push the nozzle backwards and forwards as you squeeze before releasing the pressure.

PIPED BELLS

These must be left for at least 24 hours to dry completely. Use a plain no 2 or 3 writing nozzle on an icing bag filled with royal icing and pipe large beads about 1.5 cm/¾ inch across on to waxed paper or non-stick baking parchment. Leave to dry for several hours, then pipe a small bead on top and pull the nozzle away quickly to make a thin peak which should fall over to make a loop. Use a pin to tuck in the end of the loop. Leave the bells to dry for 24 hours, then carefully peel them away from the paper and leave them to dry on their sides for a further 24 hours. Carefully scrape away the soft icing inside each with the end of a small pointed knife. Arrange the bells in pairs on the cake.

TIPS FOR SUCCESS WITH PIPED DECORATIONS

■ Make sure that the icing bag is strong.

■ Check that the icing is of the right consistency by piping a sample shape.

■ Always make plenty of extra piped decorations to allow for breakages and so that only the best ones can be used on the cake.

■ Leave the piped decorations to dry completely before removing them from the paper.

Piping Bells

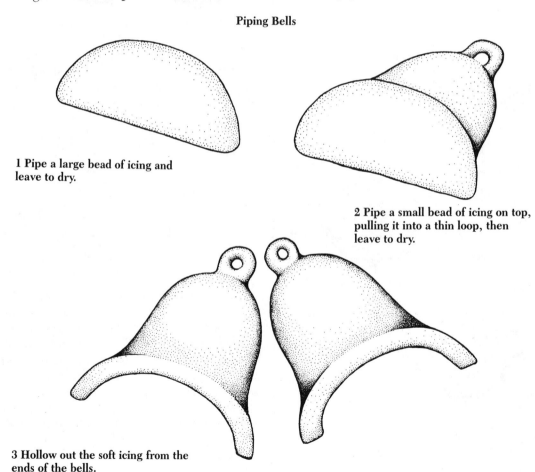

1 Pipe a large bead of icing and leave to dry.

2 Pipe a small bead of icing on top, pulling it into a thin loop, then leave to dry.

3 Hollow out the soft icing from the ends of the bells.

Easter Cakes (page 133)

Harvest Cake (page 133) decorated with marzipan fruits with marzipan vegetables nearby

Bell Cake (page 134)

Feathered Square (page 137)

Sailing Yacht (page 137)

Teddy Bear (page 138) and Novelty Buns (page 141)

Number Six Cake (page 139) and Building Blocks (page 141)

Clown Cake (page 140)

Piping Birds

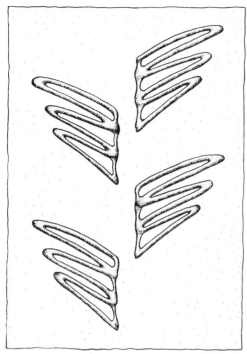

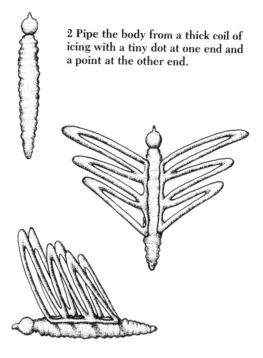

2 Pipe the body from a thick coil of icing with a tiny dot at one end and a point at the other end.

1 Pipe the wings on to waxed paper, making sure that all the feather shapes are joined at the base of the wing. Leave to dry.

3 Place a wing on either side of the body and hold in place, or support, until firm. Leave to dry.

PIPED BIRDS

These are ideal for decorating christening and wedding cakes. The wings are piped on to waxed paper, then dried before being assembled on to the body.

The icing should be of a firm peak consistency. Use an icing bag fitted with a plain no 1 or 2 writing nozzle. Line a tray with waxed paper. Hold the nozzle at an angle of 45 degrees to the paper and squeeze the icing out into a thin thread, moving the nozzle quickly backwards and forwards to the right. Pipe an arched line about 2 cm/¾ inch long, then pipe back to the starting point. This forms the first feather of the wing. Make two more feathers immediately under the first, and joined at the base, each one slightly shorter than the preceding one. This makes one wing.

Pipe several more wings over the paper, then reverse the direction and pipe the left wings. Leave the wings to dry for 24 hours.

To Assemble the Birds When the wings are dry, ease them off the paper and place them on a saucer.

Using a bag fitted with a no 2 nozzle, pipe a thick body about 2 cm/¾ inch long. Squeeze out the icing and rotate the nozzle to form a coil of icing as you slowly pull it along. Narrow the icing to a point at one end for the tail. Place a wing on either side of the body and hold them in the icing for a few seconds to set. Alternatively, support the wings in position by placing cotton wool balls under them while they dry. Pipe a small bead for the head and quickly draw away the nozzle to make a beak. When dry, the birds can be stored in the same way as the flowers.

CHOCOLATE WORK

Dark and bitter, smooth and milky or pale and creamy – there are many types of chocolate available now and they can be put to a variety of uses. This chapter explains all about chocolate, from successful melting to creative ideas for piping, shaping and curling.

CHOCOLATE AND ITS USES

Chocolate is a blend of cocoa solids and cocoa butter to which varying quantities of vegetable fats, milk and sugar have been added. The quantity of added fat determines the hardness or softness of the chocolate.

A block of chocolate can be finely or coarsely grated, chopped, slivered and curled for decorating or coating the sides and tops of cakes.

Melted chocolate is malleable; it dries to a smooth, glossy film. It flavours and provides texture, as well as setting quality, to icings and fillings. Melted chocolate has many other uses: it can be poured over cakes or fruits or marzipan and nuts can be dipped in it. Chocolate leaves are made by coating real leaves. Chocolate curls, known as caraque, are a widely used decoration. Melted chocolate can also be set in a thin sheet, then cut into shapes, for example squares, triangles or shapes using cutters. The melted chocolate can also be piped in many ways.

Milk and Plain Chocolate Milk Chocolate has added milk products and is paler and softer in texture than plain chocolate which is darker and more brittle. The quantity of added sugar determines the sweetness. Milk chocolate contains more sugar than plain chocolate which is available as bitter, semi-sweet or plain.

Chocolate-flavoured Cake Covering This is not true chocolate. In this product the cocoa butter is replaced by other fats which make it more malleable. The resulting flavour is poor and the texture waxy. It is useful for inexpensive, everyday cakes but it should not be applied when a good result is required.

White Chocolate This is made from cocoa butter, sugar and milk and does not contain any of the cocoa solids or non-fat parts of the cocoa bean.

Carob This is manufactured from the pulp of the carob or locust bean to resemble chocolate in appearance. It is naturally sweeter than cocoa so less sugar is added; also, it is caffeine free. It is in powder form for cooking and in block form for eating. Carob can be used instead of chocolate for some of the following ideas but it is waxy in consistency and does not have such a glossy appearance.

STORING CHOCOLATE DECORATIONS

Store chocolate decorations in a cool, dry atmosphere for the shortest possible time, and no longer than seven to ten days. The chocolate will sweat if it is kept in a warm room. On very hot days keep the chocolate in the refrigerator but bring it to room temperature before melting it.

CHOCOLATE ICINGS AND DECORATIONS

Use a hard, plain dessert chocolate for the best flavour and texture. Do not be disappointed by its appearance; it will not have the same high gloss as commercial chocolates. Avoid handling the chocolate once it has set as fingermarks will readily show and the surface will become dull.

CHOPPING CHOCOLATE

Break the chocolate into pieces and place it on a chopping board. Use a sharp knife with a long blade and hold the tip of the knife on to the board with one hand. Pivot the blade, bringing it up and down with the other hand. Scrape the chocolate back to the centre of the board and continue until the pieces are even and quite small.

GRATING CHOCOLATE

Place the grater on a piece of greaseproof paper on a large plate or chopping board. Rub the block of chocolate on the coarse side of the grater. Use long, even strokes and keep your hands as cool as possible.

CHOCOLATE SLIVERS

Hold your hands under cold running water, then dry them. Hold the chocolate in the palm of the hand and shave off thin pieces of chocolate with a potato peeler, letting them fall on to a chilled plate or a sheet of greaseproof paper.

MELTING CHOCOLATE

Break up or roughly chop the chocolate and place it in a basin that fits over a saucepan. Place about 5 cm/2 inches of water in the pan and bring to the boil, then remove the pan from the heat and stand the basin over it. Leave for a few minutes, then stir the chocolate until it has melted and is smooth and glossy. If you leave the pan on the heat, the chocolate will overheat and white streaks may appear in it when it sets again.

DIPPING FOOD IN CHOCOLATE

Biscuits, choux buns, nuts, marzipan shapes, real leaves and fruits such as maraschino cherries, grapes, raisins, dates and slices of banana can all be dipped in melted chocolate. They can be part-dipped or fully dipped according to the effect required. Special dipping forks have two long prongs that are bent at the ends to stop the food falling off when dipped. Alternatively, use a corn-on-the-cob fork, cocktail stick or two fine skewers, one on either side of the food. For larger pieces of food such as choux buns, or hard foods such as almonds, it is best to use your fingers to dip the ingredients.

Melt the chocolate following the instructions left. For dipping food the consistency should be thick enough to coat the back of a spoon. If the chocolate is too thin, remove the basin from the pan and leave it to cool slightly, until the chocolate thickens. Keep the chocolate warm (over the saucepan of water), while you are working. If the chocolate becomes too thick, remove the basin, re-heat the water, then replace the basin. Stir the chocolate occasionally as you are dipping the food; this gives a glossy finish.

You will need a good depth of melted chocolate to dip food successfully; it should be at least 5 cm/2 inches deep. (When the chocolate becomes too shallow for successful dipping, do not discard it; stir the excess into buttercreams or similar icings to avoid wastage.)

Line a baking sheet or wire rack with a sheet of waxed paper or non-stick baking parchment. Have ready all the food to be dipped and start with firm items, such as nuts and marzipan. Finish with soft foods, such as fruits. Plunge the food into the chocolate to the depth required, then quickly withdraw at the same angle at which it was plunged. Do not rotate part-dipped food in the chocolate or the top line of chocolate will be uneven.

Gently shake the food to allow the excess chocolate to fall back into the basin, then place it on the prepared sheet or rack to dry.

TO DIP LEAVES

Use clean, dry leaves, such as rose leaves, and brush the underside of the leaf over the surface of the chocolate. Dry the leaves chocolate side uppermost, then carefully peel away the leaf, leaving the impression of the leaf on the chocolate.

PIPING CHOCOLATE

When adding chocolate decoration to the top of a cake, melted chocolate is difficult to pipe because it begins to set in the nozzle. Mixing a little icing sugar with it will make it more malleable; however this is not suitable for piping shapes that have to set hard.

25 g/1 oz icing sugar, sifted
100 g/4 oz chocolate, melted

Stir the icing sugar into the melted chocolate with a few drops of water to make a mixture of a thick piping consistency that drops from the spoon.

MRS BEETON'S TIP If using piping chocolate in large quantities to pipe shells around a cake, use sugar syrup (page 31) instead of icing sugar to soften the chocolate.

PIPING WITH CHOCOLATE

The chocolate should be of a thin flowing consistency. Very little pressure is required to pipe with chocolate as it should flow slowly out of the bag without any encouragement.

TO DRIZZLE CHOCOLATE OVER CAKES AND BISCUITS

Place 15 ml/1 tbsp of melted chocolate into a small paper icing bag. Snip off the end and quickly move the bag backwards and forwards over the cake or biscuit. Finish by lowering the bag and quickly withdrawing it.

TO PIPE MOTIFS AND SHAPES

Prepare the pattern and piping surface as for royal icing run-outs (page 88). Alternatively, work freehand on to the waxed paper. Make several paper icing bags out of non-stick baking parchment – greaseproof paper is not strong enough for chocolate work.

Place 30-45 ml/2-3 tbsp melted chocolate in an icing bag and snip off the end. Start with a fine hole until you have checked the size of the piping. It is a good idea to practise piping beads and buttons on the paper first. Hold the bag and pipe the shapes as for run-outs (page 88) and lace (page 84). Remember to make sure that all the lines of piping are joined somewhere in the design. Shapes may be filled in using a different coloured chocolate, such as milk chocolate or white chocolate with plain chocolate. Leave the shapes to dry hard before peeling them off the waxed paper.

TO PIPE CHOCOLATE SHELLS AROUND A CAKE

Prepare piping chocolate (left). Use a strong bag made from double non-stick baking parchment and fitted with a small star nozzle. Pipe a shell pattern quickly around the cake as for royal icing (page 91). This method can also be used to pipe around home-made Easter eggs.

Outlines to Pipe in Chocolate

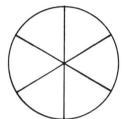

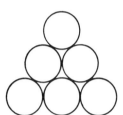

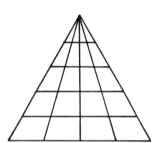

Designs to Pipe and Flood in Chocolate

TO MAKE CURLS, FRILLS AND SHAPES

Melted chocolate can be used to make a variety of different decorations without the need for piping. Here are a few examples: the key to success is to make sure that you use good quality chocolate and to leave the decorations to set firmly before using them.

CHOCOLATE CURLS OR SCROLLS (CARAQUE)

Whether you are making curls or frills the chocolate is prepared in the same way: pour melted chocolate over a clean, dry surface, such as a marble slab or a clean smooth area of work surface. Spread the chocolate backwards and forwards with a large palette knife until it is smooth, fairly thin and even. Leave to dry until almost set; do not allow the chocolate to set hard.

Hold a long, thin-bladed knife at an acute angle to the chocolate. Hold the top of the knife with the other hand and pull the knife towards you with a gentle sawing action, scraping off a thin layer of chocolate which should curl into a roll.

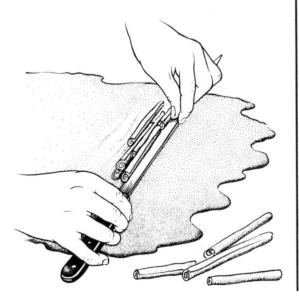

CHOCOLATE FRILLS

Starting at the edge of the chocolate, hold the tip of a small palette knife at an angle of 45 degrees or lower to the surface, and push the palette knife away from you. A thin layer of chocolate will frill as you push. Place the frills on waxed paper as you make them.

TO CUT CHOCOLATE SHAPES

Spread the melted chocolate on to waxed paper or non-stick baking parchment paper. Use petits fours cutters or small biscuit cutters, to stamp shapes out of the chocolate, cutting them as close together as possible. Leave to set hard before peeling away the paper. The excess chocolate can be finely chopped for decorations or melted for use in making more shapes.

TO CUT SQUARES, TRIANGLES OR WEDGES

Prepare a precise pattern, drawing a large square and dividing it up into smaller squares or triangles. Alternatively, draw a circle and divide it into equal wedges. In either case extend the lines beyond the square or circle so that when the pattern has been covered in chocolate, the ends of the lines will still be visible. Place the pattern under non-stick baking parchment as for royal icing run-outs (page 88).

Spread the melted chocolate over the marked shape and leave to set but not harden. Use a long-bladed knife and cut the chocolate into the shapes by holding the tip of the knife at one side of the chocolate and firmly lowering the handle so that the blade follows the cutting line. Leave the chocolate until firm, then carefully peel the shapes off the parchment.

CHOCOLATE CAKE COVERINGS

As well as chocolate-flavoured buttercreams and icings, here are two recipes for contrasting cake coverings. The Chocolate Velvet Cream recipe gives a soft and creamy, chocolate-flavoured covering that can be spread or piped on to the cake.

Alternatively, the Tipsy Chocolate Velvet is a rich, glossy and dark icing which is poured over the cake.

CHOCOLATE VELVET CREAM

150 ml/¼ pint double cream
100 g/4 oz chocolate, chopped

Combine the cream and chocolate in a small saucepan. Place over a low heat until the chocolate has melted. Continue to stir over the low heat for a further 5 minutes until the mixture is dark and creamy. Pour the cream into a bowl and chill for at least 1 hour.

Beat the cream for 5 minutes or beat it with a balloon whisk for about 10 minutes, until it has doubled in volume.

SUFFICIENT TO COVER THE TOP AND SIDES OF A 20 CM/8 INCH CAKE

TIPSY CHOCOLATE VELVET

75 g/3 oz chocolate, cut up
100 g/4 oz icing sugar, sifted
15 ml/1 tbsp dark rum
5 ml/1 tsp vegetable oil

Melt the chocolate with the 60 ml/4 tbsp water in a basin over a saucepan of hot water. Gradually beat in the icing sugar, rum and oil until the icing is smooth and coats the back of the spoon. Pour the icing over a cake and level the top and sides with a palette knife.

SUFFICIENT TO COAT THE TOP AND SIDES OF A 20 CM/8 INCH CAKE

VARIATIONS

ORANGE CHOCOLATE VELVET Use Grand Marnier instead of rum.

MOCHA VELVET Replace the rum and water with freshly made black coffee.

CAKE DESIGNS

This chapter offers a selection of ideas for elaborately decorated cakes as well as jolly novelty cakes. Any plain cake recipe of your choice can be used as a base or the recipes given here may be followed; however, the cake baked in a roasting tin (below) is most suitable for cutting into novelty shapes.

BASIC SPONGE CAKE

275 g/10 oz soft margarine
275 g/10 oz caster sugar
5 eggs, beaten
275 g/10 oz self-raising flour
7.5 ml/1½ tsp baking powder

Grease and line an oblong roasting tin measuring about 30 x 20 cm/12 x 8 inches or a 25 cm/10 inch square tin. Set the oven at 190°C/375°F/gas 5.

Place all the ingredients in a bowl. Add 15 ml/1 tbsp hot water and beat hard for 2 minutes if using an electric mixer or longer if beating by hand. The mixture should be light and creamy. It should have a soft dropping consistency.

Spoon the mixture into the prepared tin, making sure that it is spread well into the corners. Bake for 30-35 minutes until set and beginning to shrink from the sides of the tin. Turn the cake out on to a wire rack to cool.

MAKES ONE 30 x 20 CM/12 x 8 INCH CAKE OR ONE 25 CM/10 INCH SQUARE CAKE

VARIATIONS

SANDWICH CAKE Use 100 g/4 oz each of soft margarine, caster sugar and self-raising flour. Add 5 ml/1 tsp baking powder, 2 beaten eggs and a few drops of milk. Follow the method above but bake in two 18 cm/7 inch sandwich tins for 25-30 minutes.

CRYSTAL MADEIRA CAKE

225 g/8 oz butter, softened
225 g/8 oz caster sugar
grated rind and juice of 1 lemon
4 eggs, beaten
75 g/3 oz ground almonds
75 g/3 oz glacé cherries (red, green and yellow), chopped
75 g/3 oz crystallised ginger, chopped
75 g/3 oz crystallised pineapple, chopped
75 g/3 oz flaked almonds, chopped
350 g/12 oz self-raising flour

Line and grease a 25 cm/10 inch square tin. Set the oven at 180°C/350°F/gas 4.

Cream the butter, sugar and lemon rind in a mixing bowl, until light and fluffy, then beat in the eggs, a little at a time. Mix the ground almonds, cherries, ginger, pineapple and nuts together in a separate bowl, then fold the mixture into the cake, alternating with the flour until all the ingredients are incorporated. Add the lemon juice.

Spoon the mixture in the prepared tin, spreading it well into the corners. Bake for 1 hour or until the cake is firm on top and beginning to shrink from the sides. Leave to cool in the tin for 15 minutes, then turn the cake out on to a wire rack. Leave the paper on the cake.

MAKES ONE 25 CM/10 INCH SQUARE CAKE

SWISS ROLL

fat for greasing
3 eggs
75 g/3 oz caster sugar
75 g/3 oz plain flour
2.5 ml/½ tsp baking powder
pinch of salt
about 60 ml/4 tbsp jam for filling
caster sugar for dusting

Line and grease a 20 x 30 cm/8 x 12 inch Swiss roll tin. Set the oven at 220°C/425°F/gas 7.

Combine the eggs and sugar in a heat-proof bowl. Set the bowl over a pan of hot water, taking care that the bottom of the bowl does not touch the water. Whisk for 10-15 minutes until thick and creamy, then remove from the pan and continue whisking until the mixture is cold.

Sift the flour, baking powder and salt into a bowl, then lightly fold into the egg mixture. Pour into the prepared tin and bake for 10 minutes. Meanwhile warm the jam in a small saucepan.

When the cake is cooked, turn it on to a large sheet of greaseproof paper dusted with caster sugar. Peel off the lining paper. Trim off any crisp edges. Spread the cake with the warmed jam and roll up tightly from one long side. Dredge with caster sugar and place on a wire rack, with the join underneath, to cool.

MAKES ONE 30 CM/12 INCH SWISS ROLL

CHOCOLATE ROLL

fat for greasing
3 eggs
75 g/3 oz caster sugar
65 g/2½ oz plain flour
30 ml/2 tbsp cocoa
2.5 ml/½ tsp baking powder
pinch of salt
Chocolate Buttercream (pages 24-25) for
    filling
caster sugar for dusting

Line and grease a 20 x 30 cm/8 x 12 inch Swiss roll tin. Set the oven at 220°C/425°F/gas 7.

Combine the eggs and sugar in a heat-proof bowl. Set the bowl over a pan of hot water, taking care that the bottom of the bowl does not touch the water. Whisk for 10-15 minutes until thick and creamy, then remove from the pan and continue whisking until the mixture is cold.

Sift the flour, cocoa, baking powder and salt into a bowl, then lightly fold into the egg mixture. Pour into the prepared tin and bake for 10 minutes.

When the cake is cooked, turn it on to a large sheet of greaseproof paper dusted with caster sugar. Peel off the lining paper. Trim off any crisp edges. Place a second piece of greaseproof paper on top of the cake and roll up tightly from one long side, with the paper inside. Cool completely on a wire rack.

When cold, unroll carefully, spread with the buttercream and roll up again. Dust with caster sugar.

MAKES ONE 30 CM/12 INCH SWISS ROLL

ST CLEMENT'S CAKE

fat for greasing
150 g/5 oz butter or margarine
150 g/5 oz caster sugar
grated rind of 1 orange or lemon
3 eggs, beaten
150 g/5 oz self-raising flour or plain flour
    and 5 ml/1 tsp baking powder
pinch of salt
Orange or Lemon Buttercream (page 24)
    for filling
caster sugar for dredging

Line and grease two 18 cm/7 inch sandwich tins. Set the oven at 180°C/350°F/gas 4.

In a mixing bowl cream the butter or margarine with the sugar until light and fluffy. Stir in the grated citrus rind. Add the eggs gradually, beating well after each addition.

Sift the flour, salt and baking powder, if used, into a bowl. Stir into the creamed mixture, lightly but thoroughly, until evenly mixed.

Divide between the tins and bake for 25-30 minutes. Cool on a wire rack, then sandwich together with the buttercream. Sprinkle the top with caster sugar or spread with Orange or Lemon Glacé Icing (see page 27).

MAKES ONE 18 CM/7 INCH CAKE

THREE TIERED WEDDING CAKE

If possible, prepare the three tiers together, using a very large bowl. Cream the butter and sugar, and mix in the other ingredients by hand. Few ovens are large enough to bake all the tiers simultaneously; leave the cake(s) awaiting baking in a cool place overnight if necessary.

Make the cakes at least two months before covering and icing them with almond paste and royal icing. For instructions on icing and decorating the cakes, see pages 126 and 127.

When cool, the outside of each tier may be pricked with a skewer and sprinkled with brandy. To store, wrap in clean greaseproof paper and a clean tea-towel, and keep in a cool, dry place.

If the top tier of a wedding cake is to be kept for some time, fresh almond paste and royal icing should be applied when it is used.

SMALL TIER
    fat for greasing
    100 g/4 oz currants
    100 g/4 oz sultanas
    100 g/4 oz seedless raisins
    50 g/2 oz glacé cherries, chopped
    25 g/1 oz blanched whole almonds,
        chopped
    25 g/1 oz cut mixed peel
    grated rind of 1 small orange
    30 ml/2 tbsp brandy
    100 g/4 oz plain flour
    1.25 ml/¼ tsp salt
    2.5 ml/½ tsp mixed spice
    1.25 ml/¼ tsp grated nutmeg
    100 g/4 oz butter
    100 g/4 oz soft dark brown sugar
    2 large eggs, beaten
    15 ml/1 tbsp treacle
    25 g/1 oz ground almonds

Line and grease a 15 cm/6 inch round or 13 cm/5 inch square cake tin. Use doubled greaseproof paper and tie a strip of doubled brown paper around the outside of the tin. Set the oven at 140°C/275°F/gas 1.

Place the dried fruit in a bowl, removing any stalks. Add the cherries, almonds, peel, orange rind and brandy and stir well. Cover and put to one side while preparing the rest of the cake mixture.

Sift the flour, salt and spices into a large bowl. In a large mixing bowl, cream the butter and sugar until pale and fluffy. Add the beaten eggs, a quarter at a time, with a little of the flour, beating thoroughly after each addition.

Using a spoon dipped in boiling water, add the treacle. Add the rest of the flour, the ground almonds and the fruit in brandy, and stir until evenly mixed. Spoon the mixture into the prepared tin and make a slight hollow in the centre. Bake for 2¾-3 hours, until firm to the touch. Cover with ungreased greaseproof paper after 1½ hours to prevent overbrowning. Cool in the tin. Leave for 24 hours before turning out.

MIDDLE TIER
   225 g/8 oz currants
   200 g/7 oz sultanas
   200 g/7 oz seedless raisins
   100 g/4 oz glacé cherries
   50 g/2 oz blanched whole almonds
   50 g/2 oz cut mixed peel
   grated rind of 1 large orange
   45 ml/3 tbsp brandy
   200 g/7 oz plain flour
   2.5 ml/½ tsp salt
   5 ml/1 tsp mixed spice
   5 ml/1 tsp grated nutmeg
   30 ml/2 tbsp treacle
   200 g/7 oz butter
   200 g/7 oz soft dark brown sugar
   4 large eggs
   50 g/2 oz ground almonds

Make as for the small tier. Bake in a prepared 20 cm/8 inch round tin or 18 cm/7 inch square tin, in an oven preheated to 140°C/275°F/gas 1 for 4-4½ hours. Cover the

top with ungreased greaseproof paper when the cake is sufficiently brown. Cool as for the small tier.

LARGE TIER
   575 g/1¼ lb currants
   450 g/1 lb sultanas
   450 g/1 lb seedless raisins
   225 g/8 oz glacé cherries
   100 g/4 oz blanched whole almonds
   100 g/4 oz cut mixed peel
   grated rind of 2 large oranges
   125 ml/4 fl oz brandy
   450 g/1 lb plain flour
   5 ml/1 tsp salt
   10 ml/2 tsp mixed spice
   10 ml/2 tsp grated nutmeg
   75 ml/5 tbsp treacle
   450 g/1 lb butter
   450 g/1 lb soft dark brown sugar
   10 large eggs
   100 g/4 oz ground almonds

Line and grease a 28 cm/11 inch round or 25 cm/10 inch square cake tin. Use doubled greaseproof paper and tie at least three bands of brown paper around the outside of the tin. Make the cake as for the small tier. Bake in an oven preheated to 140°C/275°F/gas 1 for about 5½ hours. After 2 hours cover the top with doubled greaseproof paper, and gently give the tin a quarter turn. Turn again after each 30 minutes to avoid overbrowning. Cool as for the small tier.

MAKES ONE THREE-TIER CAKE

SMALL RICH CAKES

fat for greasing (optional)
100 g/4 oz self-raising flour
pinch of salt
100 g/4 oz butter or margarine
100 g/4 oz caster sugar
2 eggs, beaten

Grease 12-14 bun tins or support an equivalent number of paper cases in dry bun tins. Set the oven at 180°C/350°F/gas 4. Mix the flour and salt in a bowl.

In a mixing bowl, cream the butter or margarine with the sugar until light and fluffy. Beat in the eggs, then lightly stir in the flour and salt.

Divide the mixture evenly between the prepared paper cases or bun tins, and bake for 15-20 minutes until golden brown. Cool on a wire rack.

MAKES 12 TO 14

VARIATIONS

CHERRY CAKES Add 50 g/2 oz chopped glacé cherries with the flour.
CHOCOLATE CAKES Add 30 ml/2 tbsp cocoa with the flour and add 15 ml/1 tbsp milk.
COCONUT CAKES Add 50 g/2 oz desiccated coconut with the flour and 15-30 ml/1-2 tbsp milk with the eggs.
COFFEE CAKES Dissolve 10 ml/2 tsp instant coffee in 5 ml/1 tsp boiling water. Add with the eggs.
QUEEN CAKES Add 100 g/4 oz currants with the flour.

RICH CAKE

fat for greasing
200 g/7 oz plain flour
1.25 ml/¼ tsp salt
2.5 ml/½ tsp baking powder
150 g/5 oz butter or margarine
150 g/5 oz caster sugar
4 eggs, beaten
15 ml/1 tbsp milk (optional)

Line and grease a 15 cm/6 inch cake tin. Set the oven at 180°C/350°F/gas 4.

Sift the flour, salt and baking powder into a bowl. Place the butter or margarine in a mixing bowl and beat until very soft. Add the sugar and cream together until light and fluffy. Add the beaten eggs gradually, beating well after each addition. If the mixture shows signs of curdling, add a little flour.

Fold in the dry ingredients lightly but thoroughly, adding the milk if too stiff.

Spoon into the prepared tin, smooth the surface and make a hollow in the centre. Bake for 30 minutes, then reduce the oven temperature to 160°C/325°F/gas 3 and bake for 50 minutes more until firm to the touch. Cool on a wire rack.

MAKES ONE 15 CM/6 INCH CAKE

VARIATIONS

CORNFLOUR CAKE Use a mixture of equal parts cornflour and plain flour.
GROUND RICE CAKE Use a mixture of 150 g/5 oz plain flour and 50 g/2 oz ground rice.
LEMON OR ORANGE CAKE Add the grated rind of 2 lemons or oranges and use fruit juice instead of milk.

INGREDIENTS FOR RICH FRUIT CAKE

ROUND SQUARE	15 cm/6 inch 13 cm/5 inch	18 cm/7 inch 15 cm/6 inch	20 cm/8 inch 18 cm/7 inch	23 cm/9 inch 20 cm/8 inch	25 cm/10 inch 23 cm/9 inch	28 cm/11 inch 25 cm/10 inch	30 cm/12 inch 28 cm/11 inch	33 cm/13 inch 30 cm/12 inch
Currants	225 g/8 oz	275 g/10 oz	400 g/14 oz	500 g/1 lb 2oz	575 g/1¼ lb	675 g/1½ lb	900 g/2 lb	1.25 kg/2½ lb
Raisins	100 g/4 oz	150 g/5 oz	200 g/7 oz	250 g/9 oz	300 g/11 oz	375 g/13 oz	450 g/1 lb	575 g/1¼ lb
Sultanas	100 g/4 oz	150 g/5 oz	200 g/7 oz	250 g/9 oz	300 g/11 oz	375 g/13 oz	450 g/1 lb	575 g/1¼ lb
Butter, softened	100 g/4 oz	150 g/5 oz	200 g/7 oz	250 g/9 oz	300 g/11 oz	375 g/13 oz	450 g/1 lb	575 g/1¼ lb
Moist dark brown sugar	100 g/4 oz	150 g/5 oz	200 g/7 oz	250 g/9 oz	300 g/11 oz	375 g/13 oz	450 g/1 lb	575 g/1¼ lb
Lemon, grated rind of	½	½	1	1	1½	1½	2	2
Almonds, shelled	25 g/1 oz	25 g/1 oz	40 g/1½ oz	65 g/2½ oz	75 g/3 oz	90 g/3½ oz	100 g/4 oz	100 g/4 oz
Citrus peel, chopped	25 g/1 oz	25 g/1 oz	40 g/1½ oz	65 g/2½ oz	75 g/3 oz	90 g/3½ oz	100 g/4 oz	100 g/4 oz
Glacé cherries	50 g/2 oz	50 g/2 oz	75 g/3 oz	90 g/3½ oz	100 g/4 oz	150 g/5 oz	175 g/6 oz	175 g/6 oz
Plain flour	100 g/4 oz	150 g/5 oz	200 g/7 oz	250 g/9 oz	300 g/11 oz	375 g/13 oz	450 g/1 lb	575 g/1¼ lb
Ground mixed spice	1.25 ml/¼ tsp	2.5 ml/½ tsp	2.5 ml/½ tsp	5 ml/1 tsp	5 ml/1 tsp	7.5 ml/1½ tsp	7.5 ml/1½ tsp	10 ml/2 tsp
Eggs, beaten	2	2	3	4	5	6	8	10
Black treacle	10 ml/2 tsp	10 ml/2 tsp	15 ml/1 tbsp	15 ml/1 tbsp	22.5 ml/4½ tsp	22.5 ml/4½ tsp	30 ml/2 tbsp	30 ml/2 tbsp

This chart provides an alternative to the recipe for the three-tiered wedding cake on page 122. It also gives quantities for cakes of different sizes.

Set the oven at 150°C/300°F/gas 2. Line and grease the appropriate tin. Mix the currants, raisins and sultanas. Cream the butter, sugar and lemon rind until very soft. Beat in the almonds and the citrus peel. Wash and dry the cherries, then roughly chop them and toss them with a little of the measured flour. Sift the remaining flour with the spice and toss a little with the mixed dried fruit. Beat the eggs and treacle into the creamed mixture, adding a spoonful of the flour occasionally to prevent the mixture curdling. Fold in the remaining flour. Lastly fold in the fruit and the cherries.

Turn the mixture into the tin and smooth the top with the back of a wetted metal spoon, hollowing out the centre slightly. The cooking time depends on the size of the cake. The small cakes will take about 1½-2 hours, the cakes of between 20-23 cm/8-9 inches will need about 4-5 hours and the larger cakes take about 7-8 hours. Insert a clean metal skewer into the centre of the cake to test if it is cooked: it should come out clean when the cake is ready. If there is any sticky mixture on the skewer the cake is not cooked.

Leave the cake to cool in the tin for at least an hour, then transfer it to a wire rack to cool completely. Do not remove the lining paper. Wrap the cake, still in the lining paper, in fresh greaseproof paper and store it in an airtight tin.

WEDDING CAKES

Traditional tiered wedding cakes are covered in royal icing. However, sugar paste, a soft icing which is now very popular, can also be used on wedding cakes. The only minor drawback with using sugar paste is that the tiers have to be supported independently, otherwise the weight of the cake pushes the pillars into the sugar paste.

To ensure that a tiered cake looks in proportion when stacked, the size of the tiered cakes usually decreases by 5 cm/2 inches when there are three or more tiers. For a two-tier cake, the top cake may be 7.5 cm/3 inches smaller than the one below. When planning the cake, the height of any decoration on the top tier must also be considered. The cake at the base of a triple tier should be slightly deeper than the other cakes, this may be achieved by baking a 28 cm/11 inch cake quantity in a 25 cm/10 inch cake tin (see page 142).

CAKE BOARDS AND PILLARS

Cake Boards Always use drum boards for tiered cakes. The base board should be 5 cm/ 2 inches larger than the cake that stands upon it; the tiers above should have boards about 2.5 cm/1 inch larger than their cakes. If the cake is decorated with a Garrett frill or extension work, use a board which is 2.5 cm/ 1 inch larger than usual to protect the edging. Board edging or ribbon can be placed around the edges of the board. Upper cakes that are assembled directly on top of each other should be placed on thin cake cards exactly the same size as the iced cake.

Pillars Use four pillars for each tier, except for very small cakes or heart-shaped cakes when three pillars will be sufficient. Check that the pillars are all level. Make sure that the pillars are evenly positioned before assembling the tiers. It is a good idea to include the pillars on the base cake as part of the decoration design.

If the cake is covered with sugar paste, use special pillars with stakes that are pushed down through the cake to support the tiers. Alternatively, use hollow pillars and push a piece of wooden dowel through each pillar and the cake to the board. It is important to measure the length of dowel required accurately, otherwise the weight of the cake will rest on the pillars, rather than on the lengths of dowel. If the dowel rods are too long, or if they are uneven, the tiers will not be level.

TIMING

Making the Cakes The cakes should be made at least three months in advance. They should be wrapped in several layers of greaseproof paper, then in foil, and stored in a cool, dry place. *Do not* wrap cakes in cling film as they tend to sweat. Nor should cakes be wrapped directly in foil since the acid in the fruit would react with aluminium and the foil would disintegrate in particles on the surface of the cake.

The Almond Paste Use white almond paste and leave this to dry on the cake for at least 2 weeks. Cover the cake layers lightly with a clean tea-towel or greaseproof paper to protect them from dust.

The Icing Allow at least 2 weeks for the completed flat icing to dry before adding any piping and decoration.

Cutting the Cake The cake should be cut into pieces about 5 cm/2 inches by 2.5 cm/1 inch. Cut right across the cake, making large 2.5 cm/1 inch thick slices. Cut the slices into fingers. Remember that you will cut fewer pieces from a round cake than from a square one. If a large number of guests are to be entertained and lots of cake is to be posted out, it is a good idea to bake an additional large square cake and cover it with almond paste and icing. There is no need to add decorations, but the extra cake can then be cut up behind the scenes and served as required.

THREE-TIERED WEDDING CAKE

Illustrated on page 33

The cake is covered in royal icing and decorated with garlands of piped roses in pastel shades. Instead of flowers, run-outs of hearts, bells, birds or the couple's initials can be used to decorate the sides of the cakes. The decoration on this cake can be used with the recipe for the alternative Three-tiered Wedding Cake given on page 122.

3 square Rich Fruit Cakes (page 125), covered with Almond Paste (page 22) and flat iced with Royal Icing (page 32):
    1 x 25 cm/10 inch
    1 x 20 cm/8 inch
    1 x 15 cm/6 inch
about 800 g/1¾ lb Royal Icing (page 32), for piping

DECORATION

240 piped roses (page 102):
    80 pastel pink
    80 pastel green
    80 cream
(this number allows plenty of choice)
piped green leaves (page 103)

NOZZLES

plain writing nozzle no 1
small star nozzle
medium shell or star nozzle

All three cakes should be flat iced, on cake boards ready for decorating. Draw and cut out the following circles in thin white card: one 18 cm/7 inches in diameter, one 13 cm/5 inches in diameter and one 7.5 cm/3 inches in diameter. Divide each circle into four equal segments and cut out one quarter segment from each to use as a template.

Place the largest template on the corner of the bottom cake and gently scratch around the curved edge with a pin. Repeat with the remaining corners. Mark curves on the corners of the smaller cakes in the same way, each time using the appropriate sized template as guide.

Using an icing bag fitted with the plain nozzle, pipe double trellis work in royal icing over the marked corner areas of each cake. Neaten the trellis by piping a row of fine stars using a second bag fitted with the small star nozzle on the curved edges.

Cut paper patterns to fit one side of each cake. Fold the larger piece of paper into three and the second piece into two. Mark a line 1 cm/½ inch from the top and 1 cm/½ inch from the bottom of each folded pattern and along the pattern for the smallest cake. Draw around a tea cup or similar round object to make a curve between the lines on the patterns. Cut round the curve, open out the folded paper and transfer the patterns on to pieces of thin white card. The largest cake should have three scallops along its side, the middle cake two scallops and the smallest cake one curve only (page 142).

Position the patterns on the sides of the cakes and prick the scallop designs on to the icing with a pin or fine skewer.

Using an icing bag fitted with the medium shell or star nozzle, pipe a row of shells around the top and lower edges of the cakes. Stick the roses, in alternate colours along the marked pattern on the sides of the cake. Make sure you have flowers of the same colour at the top of each curve on each side of the cakes, so that all three tiers match. Position three or more roses on top of each cake between the trellis work and one rose in each corner on the shell edging. Place the green leaves at random between the roses.

ABOUT 120 PORTIONS

SINGLE-TIER WEDDING CAKE

Illustrated on page 34

If you do not want to attempt the complicated extension work on this cake, simply pipe a border of shells on the cake.

30 cm/12 inch Rich Fruit Cake (page 125), covered with Almond Paste (page 22)
Sugar Paste (page 42) tinted with cream colouring
450 g/1 lb Royal Icing (page 32), for piping

DECORATION

2 m/6½ feet x 5 mm/¼ inch cream ribbon
selection of frosted flowers (page 49)

NOZZLES

plain writing nozzles nos 2 and 0

The cake should be positioned on a 38 cm/ 15 inch round cake board. Using the no 0 nozzle pipe embroidery over the cake, leaving the centre area free, as shown in the photograph (page 34).

Place the ribbon around the cake and secure it at the back of the cake. Pipe extension work around the base of the cake, below the ribbon, omitting the initial line of shells (page 86). Neaten the top edge with a row of tiny beads. Leave the icing to dry.

The day before the wedding plan an arrangement of frosted flowers on a board, then carefully transfer it to the cake, taking care not to touch – and therefore damage – the extension work.

ABOUT 60 PORTIONS

CHRISTENING CAKES

These can be iced in royal icing or in sugar paste and the sugar paste can be used on a rich sponge cake instead of a fruit cake if preferred.

Traditionally, for a Christening, cakes were round and iced in blue for a boy and pink for a girl. Although this tradition is often followed, many new ideas are now used instead. For example, a cake baked in the shape of the initial letter of the child's name makes an interesting centrepiece. Cake tins in the shape of letters and numerals are available for hire from special cake decorating shops, some bakers and kitchen shops. Check that the tin will be available when you need it as most are only hired for 48 hours. This means you have to be ready to make and cook the cake to time. It is not a good idea to cut your own shape from fruit cakes, as once cut, the cake tends to dry more quickly.

CAKE TIN SIZES

Unless an initial tin comes with instructions and a guide to quantities, you will need to use the capacity test to work out the quantity of cake mixture to use. Measure the quantity of water needed to fill the tin, then pour this water into a round or square cake tin until you find one where the water equals the height of a cooked cake. Generally speaking, initial cakes look best if they are quite deep.

If the chosen tin comes as a 'form' without a base, you will have to measure it and do some guesswork!

GIRL'S CHRISTENING CAKE

Illustrated on page 35

Instead of a fruit cake, a classic Madeira cake mixture can be used to make this cake, in which case it should not be covered with almond paste. The exact number of portions depends on the shape of the cake; remember that Madeira cake is cut in larger pieces than fruit cake.

Rich Fruit Cake (page 125) baked in the
    shape of an initial and covered in
    Almond Paste (page 22)
Sugar Paste, allowing about 225 g/8 oz
    more than for a round or square cake
    (page 42)
450 g/1 lb Royal Icing (page 32), for
    piping

DECORATIONS

20 small piped pink roses (page 102)
1 m/3¼ feet pink ribbon

NOZZLES

plain writing nozzle no '0'
small star or shell nozzle

Roll out small strips of sugar paste to the same depth as the cake and use to cover the insides of any holes in the letter. In the cake illustrated on page 35, the triangle below the apex of the letter is covered in this way. Smooth the top edge of the paste so that it graduates smoothly into the top of the cake.

Measure across the widest part of the cake and add on twice the depth of the cake. Roll out the icing to fit this measurement and smooth it over the cake (see Mrs Beeton's Tip). It will take some time to smooth the paste evenly around all the corners but this is necessary in order to achieve a good result. Trim and smooth the icing as you go (page 61). Leave the cake to dry for 24 hours.

Measure the height and length of one long side of the cake and cut a paper pattern to fit. Draw a line 2.5 cm/1 inch up from the base of the pattern and repeat with the shortest side. Fold the long piece into three. Using a teacup or pastry cutter mark a curve to fit each paper, cut and open out the paper. Place the paper on the cake and prick out the curves with a pin. Repeat with one curve on the leg of the letter.

Use royal icing in an icing bag fitted with a plain nozzle no 0 and pipe a cornelli pattern (page 82) over the top of the cake and down into each curve.

Using a second bag, this time with the small star nozzle, pipe small stars around the curves to make a neat border for the cornelli icing. Pipe a row of shells around the base of the cake and place a rose on the side of the cake at each point where two curves meet.

Make a flamboyant bow with the ribbon and place it on the cake as shown in the photograph.

ABOUT 40 PORTIONS

VARIATION

For letters of the alphabet that have long curves, cut the paper pattern to fit and fold an appropriate number of times to make equal curves.

> **MRS BEETON'S TIP** In the cases of shapes that are long and thin, roll the paste into a strip and gently ease this over the shape.

BOY'S CHRISTENING CAKE

Illustrated on page 36

*White run-out trains puffing around the sides of a
pale blue cake create a very effective design.*

23 cm/9 inch square Rich Fruit Cake
  (page 125), covered in Almond Paste
  (page 22)
Sugar Paste (page 42) tinted with blue
  food colouring
225 g/8 oz Royal Icing (page 32), for
  piping
blue food colouring

NOZZLES

plain writing nozzle no 1 or 2
medium shell nozzle

DECORATIONS

train run-outs (page 143), consisting of 5
  engines and 16 carriages
run-out letters (pages 88-90)

Cut out a 23 cm/9 inch square paper
pattern and a 20 cm/8 inch square paper
pattern. Centre the smaller square on top of
the larger one and draw around it to mark a
20 cm/8 inch square within the 23 cm/9 inch
square. Place the pattern on top of the cake
and mark the inner square on to the icing by
pricking pin holes fairly close together.

Place a little royal icing in an icing bag
fitted with the plain writing nozzle and pipe a
line along the square marked out on the cake
(page 81). Pipe a second line of icing inside
the first so that the lines are almost touching.

Attach the train run-outs to the sides of
the cake with a little icing and pipe large
beads for wheels and carriage links. Pipe a
swirl of smoke from each funnel. Place the
letters, and an engine, on top of the cake
attaching them with a little icing.

Use a second icing bag, with the shell
nozzle, to pipe a row of shells around the
base of the cake. Leave all the icing to dry
before moving the cake.

ABOUT 35 PORTIONS

SILVER OR GOLDEN ANNIVERSARY CAKE

25 cm/10 inch round Rich Fruit Cake
  (page 125) covered in Almond Paste
  (page 22) and Royal Icing (page 32)
225 g/8 oz Royal Icing (page 32), for
  piping

NOZZLES

plain writing nozzle no 1
medium star nozzle

DECORATIONS

1 m/3¼ feet silver or gold sequin ribbon
'25' or '50' run-out (pages 88-90)
silver or gold food colouring
piped doves (page 113)

Position the run-out on the cake. Place a
little royal icing in an icing bag fitted with the
plain writing nozzle and pipe 'congratula-
tions' underneath the run-out. When the
icing is dry, brush the edges lightly with
silver or gold colouring as shown in the
photograph. Change to an icing bag fitted
with the star nozzle and pipe a small row of
stars along the top and bottom edges of the
cake. Leave the icing to dry.

Attach the doves to the top of the cake
with little beads of white royal icing (use the
writing nozzle). Finish the cake with a
ribbon.

ABOUT 35 PORTIONS

...

RUBY ANNIVERSARY CAKE

If time is short, the edge of this cake can be finished with a twisted rope of sugar paste instead of the frill. The design can be used for silver or gold anniversary cakes by changing the colour of the roses and ribbon.

25 cm/10 inch square Rich Fruit Cake (page 125) covered with Almond Paste (page 22) and Sugar Paste (page 42)
225 g/8 oz Sugar Paste (page 42) for frill
cornflour for dusting

DECORATIONS

moulded marzipan roses (page 97) or carnations (page 98), coloured deep red
1 m/3¼ feet deep red velvet narrow ribbon
deep red and gold food colouring

The cake must be placed on a 33 cm/13 inch square board. Use some of the extra sugar paste to make a Garrett frill and attach it to the base of the cake (page 93).

Roll out the remaining paste thickly and cut out four 5 cm/2 inch circles. Mould each into an oval and leave to dry for 24 hours on a non-stick surface dusted with cornflour. With a fine paint brush and red or gold food colouring, write '40' on each oval. Using a palette knife lift the plaques on to the cakes positioning one in each corner. Outline each plaque with a little gold colouring.

Arrange the flowers in the centre of the cake and add the narrow ribbon directly above the frill to neaten it.

ABOUT 40 PORTIONS

TWENTY-FIRST BIRTHDAY CAKE

Illustrated on page 37

25 cm/10 inch quantity Rich Fruit Cake (page 125), baked in a tin about 30 cm x 20 cm/12 x 8 inches and covered in Almond Paste (page 22)
1 kg/2¼ lb Sugar Paste (page 42)
225 g/8 oz Royal Icing (page 32) for piping
navy blue or marine food colouring
navy blue or marine food colouring

NOZZLES

plain writing nozzle no 1 or 2
shell nozzle

DECORATIONS

1 m/3¼ feet ribbon, 1 cm/½ inch wide
run-out '21' in blue (pages 88-90)

The cake should be placed on a 35 x 25 cm/14 x 10 inch gold board. Cover it with the sugar paste (page 61), then insert the ribbon 2.5 cm/1 inch up from the base of the cake (page 77).

Cut out two paper rectangles, one 30 x 20 cm/12 x 8 inches, the other 25 x 15 cm/10 x 6 inches. Cut off the corners on the smaller rectangle (page 143). Lay the smaller rectangle on the larger one and draw around it. Place this pattern on the cake and mark it by pricking pin holes round it.

Using the plain writing nozzle, pipe a row of icing around the marked design. Set aside to dry. Colour a little of the remaining royal icing navy blue and, using the clean writing nozzle, pipe over the white. Change to a shell nozzle and pipe a row of white shells around the base. Fix the run-out '21' in the centre.

ABOUT 40 PORTIONS

MUSICAL NOTES BIRTHDAY CAKE

Illustrated on page 38

This cake is ideal for any birthday, particularly for an eighteenth celebration. Since it is made up of two cakes it is also a good idea for twins.

two 15 cm/6 inch round Rich Fruit Cakes
   (page 125)
18 cm/7 inch square Rich Fruit Cake
   (page 125)
1.5 kg/3 lb Almond Paste (page 22)
1 kg/2 lb Royal Icing (page 32)
black food colouring

NOZZLES

small star nozzle
plain writing nozzle no 1 or 2

Cut the square cake into two 5 cm/2 inch strips and one 7.5 cm/3 inch strip. Trim the round cakes as shown in the diagram on page 144. Cover all the cakes with almond paste (page 60).

Assemble the cake on the board, then remove the top cake only. Move the notes slightly apart, then cover them and the individual bar cake in smooth royal icing. When completely dry, slide the notes back together and place the bar cake back into position.

Colour the remaining royal icing black and place in an icing bag fitted with a small star nozzle. Pipe a small shell edging around the base and top edges of the cake.

Change to a bag fitted with the plain writing nozzle and pipe 'Happy Birthday' on the top bar. Pipe the appropriate number or name on the notes.

ABOUT 50 PORTIONS

BRUSH EMBROIDERY CAKES

Illustrated on page 39

Brush embroidery is painted directly on to the cake using a fine line of royal icing as the starting point.

Trace the pattern of the icing design from embroidery patterns, cards or other pictorial sources. Prick the shapes out on the cake. The cake covering must be dry before you do this. You may like to trace the flower or butterfly patterns on page 145. These are illustrated on finished cakes on page 39. The cakes are covered in sugar paste and finished with ribbons.

You will need about 30-45 ml/2-3 tbsp Royal Icing (page 32), made up to soft peak consistency. Stir in 1.25 ml/¼ tsp piping gel to prevent the icing from drying out too quickly (page 13). Divide the icing between two or three egg cups and colour as required. Place each colour in a paper icing bag without a nozzle.

Snip off the point from one of the icing bags and pipe an outline around one of the petals or wings. Dip a fine paint brush in water then wipe it across a clean sponge. Use the damp brush to gently pull the icing down the design using long firm strokes; work towards the centre of the flower or butterfly.

Build up the design by piping different shades of icing around the flower or wings. The piping must be completed in sections and each section allowed to dry before beginning the next. When dry, pipe in stalks or leaves and dust the pattern with petal dust or lustre.

When piping large areas, a double line of icing should be piped so that there is enough icing to pull across the area of the design.

HARVEST CAKE

Illustrated on page 106

The cake can either be covered in a thin layer of marzipan or almond paste and sugar paste; a sponge cake can be covered in buttercream. The basket weave piping is done in royal icing; however buttercream can also used.
The centre of the basket is filled with a selection of moulded marzipan fruits, vegetables and leaves (pages 101 and 95).

  23 cm/9 inch round Rich Fruit Cake (page 125) covered in Marzipan (page 22) or Almond Paste (page 22) and Sugar Paste (page 42)
  450 g/1 lb Royal Icing (page 32), tinted with yellow or cream food colouring

DECORATION

  marzipan fruits, vegetables and leaves (pages 101 and 95)

NOZZLES

  medium basket or ribbon nozzle
  plain writing nozzle no 2
  small shell or star nozzle

Centre the cake on a 28 cm/11 inch board. Cut out a 23 cm/9 inch circle of greaseproof paper and fold it in half. Draw a line parallel to the fold and 5 cm/2 inches away from it. Turn the paper over and draw another line 5 cm/2 inches from the fold. Open out the paper.

Place the pattern on top of the cake and mark the position of the two lines with a pin. Remove the pattern. Place some of the royal icing in an icing bag fitted with the basket nozzle and fill in the two end areas on top of the cake with basket weave piping (page 92). Change to an icing bag fitted with the writing nozzle and neaten the straight edges of the basket weave piping with a line of plain piping.

Pipe basket weave around the side of the cake. Using an icing bag fitted with the shell nozzle, neaten the top and bottom edges with a row of fine shells. Leave icing to dry.

Arrange the fruits, vegetables and leaves down the centre of the cake.

ABOUT 30 PORTIONS

EASTER CAKES

Illustrated on page 105

Yellow is associated with Easter and springtime and yellow almond paste or marzipan is traditionally used to cover Simnel and Easter cakes.

EASTER LOG

Cover a Swiss Roll (page 121) with yellow almond paste by first cutting out two circles to fit the ends and then enclosing in a large piece of almond paste extending slightly over the ends. Neaten the roll, then drizzle melted chocolate over the top. Decorate the board with green-coloured desiccated coconut (page 48), moulded marzipan ducks (page 100) and small Easter eggs or piped spring flowers.

EASTER CROWN

Colour almond paste green. Roll it out and cut a shape to cover the side only of a round cake (page 60). Before placing the almond paste in position around the cake, pattern it by pressing a meat hammer or grater over the surface. Coat the top of the cake in Apricot Glaze (page 20); sprinkle with chopped chocolate and lay the moulded marzipan daffodils (page 99) on top.

FATHER CHRISTMAS CAKE

Illustrated on page 40

Prepare and paint the run-out for this cake in advance, allowing it to dry before placing it on the cake. Leftover royal icing is used to pipe the beard and fur trimmings.

23 cm/9 inch square Rich Fruit Cake
    (page 125), covered in Almond Paste
    (page 22) and Royal Icing (page 32)
225 g/8 oz Royal Icing (page 32) for piping
red food colouring

NOZZLES

1 plain writing nozzle no 1
1 medium shell or star nozzle

DECORATION

run-out Father Christmas (page 148)
1.25 metres/4 feet red ribbon, about 4 cm/
    1½ inches wide

Place some of the extra royal icing in an icing bag fitted with the writing nozzle and pipe the greetings message (as shown in the photograph) on the cake. Top the Father Christmas run-out with Cornelli icing on the beard and trimmings. Leave to dry. Fit the shell nozzle on to a second bag of royal icing and pipe a border of shells or stars around the top and lower edge of the cake. Allow the icing to dry for several hours.

Stick the run-out in position and place the ribbon around the Father Christmas cake, securing it at the back.

Colour a little of the remaining royal icing red. Place it in an icing bag fitted with the clean writing nozzle and pipe directly over the white writing to highlight the greetings.

ABOUT 35-40 PORTIONS

BELL CAKE

Illustrated on page 107

Crystal Madeira Cake (page 120), baked
    in a roasting tin
Apricot Glaze (page 20)
1.25 kg/2½ lb Sugar Paste (page 42)
red and green food colourings

Trace and cut out the template (page 147) for the bell. Place the template on the cake and cut around the shape. Position the pieces on a 35 x 30 cm/14 x 12 inch board, sticking them together with apricot glaze. Brush more glaze over the whole cake. Use 900 g/2 lb of the sugar paste to cover the cake (page 61).

Divide and colour the remaining sugar paste as follows:
mould 50 g/2 oz into a clanger
colour 75 g/3 oz red
colour 75 g/3 oz green

Reserve a little red and green paste. Roll the remaining red paste into two ropes, each measuring 20 cm/8 inches long. Roll the remaining green paste into two similar ropes. Twist one green and one red rope lightly together and repeat with the other two ropes. Place the ropes across the lower half of the bell and join them in the middle in a decorative knot.

Shape the reserved red and green paste into a loop for the top of the bell. Place the clanger and loop in position.

ABOUT 60 PORTIONS

MINI CHRISTMAS CAKES

These small cakes make an ideal Christmas gift for anyone who lives alone.

20 cm/8 inch round quantity Rich Fruit
    Cake mixture (page 125)
Almond Paste (page 22)
Sugar Paste (page 42)

DECORATION

    cut-out candle, holly and berries (page
      146, lower)
    moulded snowman (page 100), without a
      scarf
    red or orange icing pen or food colouring
    red and green food colouring

You will need crimpers and a modelling tool to decorate these cakes. Use two 10 cm/ 4 inch round cake tins as containers to bake the rich fruit cake mixture. Alternatively, wash and dry two empty 822 g/1 lb 3 oz cans, for example fruit cans. Bake the cakes for about 1½ hours, leave them to cool and cover with almond paste and sugar paste.

Using the crimpers, mark around the top edge of one of the cakes (page 76). Roll out a thin rope of sugar paste and place it around the base of the cake, joining it at the back to make a neat edge.

Place the candle, holly and berries on the top of the cake. Use a dampened paint brush to moisten them if they are dry. If the cut-outs are freshly made, smooth them on to the cake and round off the corners. Leave the cake to dry.

Finish this first cake by painting or drawing short lines radiating out from the flame of the candle. Tie a ribbon around the side of the cake, if you like, securing the join at the back with a tiny piece of adhesive tape.

To decorate the second cake, use the modelling tool to mark around the top edge of the cake. Divide the remaining sugar paste in half and colour one portion red, the other green. Make the snowman's scarf by arranging two thin rolls of coloured paste side by side. Place the scarf around the snowman's neck.

Roll the remaining portions of coloured paste separately into two long rolls, twist these together lightly and place them around the lower edge of the cake. Make a decorative join at the front of the cake. Place the snowman on top of the cake.

ABOUT 10-12 PORTIONS EACH

FESTIVE LOG

Swiss Roll (page 121) or Chocolate Roll
    (page 121)
1 quantity American Frosting (page 28)

DECORATION

    Chocolate leaves (page 116) or Marzipan
      leaves (page 95), dipped in chocolate
    small piece of marzipan or moulding
      icing, coloured red and rolled into
      berries

Place the cake on a suitable board. Make up the frosting and quickly spread it over the cake, making sure it comes well down on each side. As the frosting begins to set, draw a fork or serrated scraper down the length of the cake. Swirl the icing on the ends of the cake into circles. Add the leaves and berries to complete the decoration.

ABOUT 10 PORTIONS

DARK SECRETS RING CAKE

An irresistible almond-flavoured cake, soaked in maraschino syrup and coated in dark chocolate. Maraschino cherries with stalks are available, bottled in syrup, from good food shops.

150 g/5 oz butter, softened
150 g/5 oz caster sugar
3 small eggs, beaten
200 g/7 oz self-raising flour
50 g/2 oz ground almonds
a little milk
75 ml/3 fl oz maraschino syrup (from a jar of cherries, or home-made syrup flavoured with the liqueur)
fat for greasing
flour for dusting

ICING AND DECORATION

one quantity Tipsy Chocolate Velvet (page 119), omitting the rum
icing sugar for dusting
half quantity Citrus Cheese Icing (page 51)
small star nozzle
three pairs of maraschino cherries, half dipped in plain chocolate (page 115)

Grease a 1.1 litre/2 pint capacity ring tin and dust it lightly with flour. Set the oven at 160°C/325°F/gas 3.

Cream the butter and sugar in a mixing bowl until pale and soft, then beat in the eggs, a little at a time. Fold in the flour and ground almonds, adding sufficient milk to give the mixture a soft, dropping consistency.

Spread the mixture into the prepared tin and stand it on a baking sheet. Bake the cake for 1-1¼ hours, until firm to the touch and beginning to shrink from the side of the tin.

Leave the cake to rest in the tin for 5 minutes, then turn it out on to a wire rack.

Wash and dry the mould and invert the cake back into it. Prick the cake all over with a skewer. Warm the maraschino syrup and drizzle it over the warm cake. Leave the cake to cool completely in the mould. When it is cold, invert the cake on to a piece of non-stick baking parchment on a wire rack or baking sheet. Pour the chocolate icing over the cake, using a palette knife to smooth the sides if it does not coat the cake evenly. Leave it to set, then trim the base of any excess chocolate and carefully transfer the cake to a plate. Dust with icing sugar.

Place the citrus cheese icing in an icing bag fitted with a star nozzle and pipe a row of small stars around the base of the cake. Decorate with the dipped cherries.

MRS BEETON'S TIP Instead of using the cherries for decoration, this rich ring cake can be varied by adding different decorations according to the season. For example frosted or moulded flowers may be used to decorate the cake for Easter. For a quick Christmas cake add holly leaves and berries instead of the cherries. For a fun birthday cake combine moulded flowers or shop-bought decorations with a ring of birthday candles on the top of the cake.

ABOUT 20 PORTIONS

FEATHERED SQUARE

Illustrated on page 108

A simply decorated square sponge cake – ideal as an impromptu birthday cake, for Mother's Day or just for a Sunday-tea treat!

25 cm/10 inch square Basic Sponge Cake (page 120)
Buttercream (page 24) made with 175 g/6 oz icing sugar

DECORATION

100 g/4 oz chopped pistachio nuts (or chopped mixed nuts or desiccated coconut, tinted green)
one quantity Glacé Icing (page 27)
green food colouring
small star nozzle
Piped Blossom (page 103) or bought piped flowers

Cut the cake in half horizontally, then sandwich the cake layers together with about one third of the buttercream. Spread about half the remaining buttercream around the sides of the cake. Coat the sides in the chopped nuts or coconut and place the cake on a board or plate.

Colour half the glacé icing green, place white and green glacé icing in separate paper icing bags, then feather ice the top of the cake (page 71). Place the remaining buttercream in an icing bag fitted with a star nozzle and pipe small stars around the top and bottom edges of the cake. Decorate with piped blossom or bought piped flowers.

ABOUT 25 PORTIONS

SAILING YACHT

Illustrated on page 109

Basic Sponge Cake (page 120), baked in a roasting tin
1 quantity Apricot Glaze (page 20)
575 g/1¼ lb Sugar Paste (page 42)
yellow, red and blue food colourings
1 quantity Glacé Icing (page 27)
a little icing sugar

Trace and cut out the template on page 149; place it on the cake and cut out the pieces. Arrange the cake pieces together to form a boat shape on a 35 cm/14 inch square cake board, using apricot glaze to stick them together. Brush the cake with glaze.

Halve the sugar paste and colour one half yellow. Remove a small piece from the white piece and colour it red. Cut a small piece of paste from the white portion – enough to form a thick rope 23 cm/9 inches long. Set this aside.

Roll out the remaining white paste to about 38 x 13 cm/15 x 5 inches and smooth it over the base part of the boat. Trim the excess paste from the edges of the cake.

Roll out the yellow paste to about 25 cm/10 inches square. Cut this diagonally, making one piece slightly larger than the other, then smooth it over the sails of the boat cake. Trim the edges. Shape a flag from the red paste and position it as shown in the photograph. Place the reserved white paste in position to represent a mast. Colour a little of the glacé icing red and pipe the name of the child on the boat.

Colour the remaining glacé icing blue, adding a little extra icing sugar to give the icing a stiff texture. Spread the icing roughly over the board to represent the sea.

ABOUT 25 PORTIONS

*T*EDDY BEAR

Illustrated on page 110

Basic Sponge Cake (page 120), baked in a
    roasting tin
Buttercream (page 24) made with 450 g/
    1 lb icing sugar
a little milk
50 g/2 oz Sugar Paste (page 42)
brown, black, blue and red food
    colourings
small savoy nozzle

Trace and cut out the template for the teddy bear (page 151). Place the template on the cake and cut around the shape. Place the cake pieces on a large board – at least 35 x 30 cm/14 x 12 inches – joining the paws and feet with a little of the buttercream.

Place 60 ml/4 tbsp of the remaining buttercream in a small bowl and slacken it with a little milk. Using a small palette knife, cover the whole cake, including the sides, with a thin layer of this soft buttercream.

Knead a little brown colouring into two thirds of the sugar paste, roll it out and use the template to cut out the teddy bear's paws, feet and ears. Remember to reverse the template for one paw and one foot. Press the sugar paste pieces lightly on the cake.

Colour one third of the remaining sugar paste black to make the nose. Half of the last portion of paste should be coloured blue to make the eyes and the remainder coloured red for ribbon.

Place one third of the buttercream in an icing bag fitted with a small savoy nozzle and pipe stars all over the cake, re-filling the bag as necessary. Do not press too hard or the stars will be too thick. Slacken the icing with a few drops of milk, if necessary, to make the stars softer. To finish the cake, place the paste eyes, nose and ribbon in position.

ABOUT 20 PORTIONS

*S*PIDER'S WEBS

*Children will love these individual cakes,
decorated to resemble spider's webs. They are
especially good for Hallowe'en.*

Basic Sponge Cake (page 120), baked in
    25 cm/10 inch square tin or in a
    roasting tin
200 g/7 oz bar plain chocolate
1 quantity Apricot Glaze (page 20)
1 quantity Glacé Icing (page 27)
blue food colouring

Set aside 50 g/2 oz of the chocolate and grate or finely chop the remainder. Sprinkle the grated or chopped chocolate on to a piece of greaseproof paper. Using a 5.5 cm/ 2¼ inch cutter, cut out 16 circles from the cake. Brush the sides of each piece of cake with apricot glaze, then coat them in the grated chocolate.

Place the reserved chocolate in a basin and melt it over a saucepan of hot water. Tint the glacé icing pale blue and ice the tops of the cakes. Immediately transfer the melted chocolate to a paper icing bag, snip the end and feather ice the cakes with chocolate (page 71). If you like, place a small piece of grated chocolate somewhere on the 'web' to represent a spider.

ABOUT 16 PORTIONS

NUMBER SIX CAKE

Illustrated on page 111

Cakes in the shape of numerals or letters can be baked in shaped cake tins which can be hired from cake decorating shops, kitchen shops or bakers. Alternatively, bake a basic round cake and follow the instructions for cutting the cake in the shape of the numeral.

20 cm/8 inch Basic Sponge Sandwich
    Cake (page 120)
1 quantity Apricot Glaze (page 20) or jam
900 g/2 lb Sugar Paste (page 42)
food colouring
moulded or piped flowers or moulded
    shapes or cut-outs (pages 95 and 102)

Sandwich the cake layers together with apricot glaze or jam. Trace and cut out the template for the numeral (page 150). Place the template on the cake and cut around the shapes. Cut the hole in the six using a 3 cm/1¼ inch cutter.

Assemble the pieces of cake on a 35 x 25 cm/14 x 10 inch board, sticking the pieces together with some of the apricot glaze or jam. Brush the cake with apricot glaze. Fill in any small gaps with pieces of sugar paste to make a smooth surface.

Reserve a small piece of sugar paste to make a plain rope for the base of the cake. Colour the remaining sugar paste in the colour of your choice, following the instructions on page 61.

Roll out a small piece of sugar paste to the same depth as the cake and use to cover the inside of the hole in the six. Smooth the paste edges over the top of the cake. Roll out the remaining paste to a piece large enough to cover the cake, lift it over and smooth it down, taking care to cut the paste at the hole.

Smooth the edges down to neaten them over the existing paste. Trim all excess paste as you go. Trim the edges.

Decorate the base of the cake with a fine rope shaped from the reserved sugar paste. Add the decorations to the top of the cake, as shown in the photograph.

MRS BEETON'S TIP The basic sponge cake baked in a roasting tin can be cut up to make cakes in the shape of different numerals. First cut a piece of greaseproof paper to the same size as the cake. Draw the shape of the numeral on the paper, making the most economical use of the cake to avoid wastage. When you have decided exactly how to cut the cake and how the pieces will fit together to make the numeral, cut the shape out of paper and use this as a template for cutting the shape.

ABOUT 20 PORTIONS

CLOWN CAKE

Illustrated on page 112

This cheerful fellow is easily cut from a rectangular cake following the template.

Basic Sponge Cake (page 120), cooked in
    a roasting tin
Buttercream (page 24) made with 450 g/1
    lb icing sugar
milk (see method)
225 g/8 oz Sugar Paste (page 42)
black, red, pink or flesh, green, yellow
    and brown food colourings

NOZZLES

    small ribbon or basket nozzle
    plain writing nozzle no 2

Trace the template (page 152). Place it on the cake and cut out the shapes. Place the main body pieces on a 50 x 30 cm/20 x 1 inch cake board and set the boots, hands, head and hat aside on a tray. Place 75 ml/5 tbsp of the buttercream in a small bowl and slacken it with a little milk. Spread it very thinly over all the pieces of cake, especially down the sides.

Divide the sugar paste in half, colouring one half pink.

Divide the remaining sugar paste in half and colour one piece black. Lastly divide the uncoloured sugar paste in half, colouring one piece red and the other green.

Roll out two thirds of the pink paste into an 18 cm/7 inch circle. Smooth this over the face and down the sides of the cake. Roll out the remaining pink paste to a rectangle measuring about 15 x 10 cm/6 x 4 inches and cut this in half lengthways. Smooth these pieces over the clown's hands.

Roll out the black paste into a rectangle measuring 15 x 10 cm/6 x 4 inches. Cut in half lengthways and smooth one piece over each boot. Place the pieces of cake that make up the head and hat into position.

Colour three-quarters of the remaining buttercream green. Colour 45 ml/3 tbsp of the second half brown and the remainder yellow.

Spread half the green buttercream over the lower half of the clown to represent trousers and cover his hat. Place the remainder in an icing bag fitted with the ribbon nozzle.

Spread the yellow buttercream liberally over the top half of the clown, swirling it with a knife. Place the boots and hands in position on the cake. Pipe a frill of green buttercream along the top and bottom of the trousers, on the sleeves, around the collar and around the hat. Using the same bag of buttercream, pipe a pair of braces from the trousers to the shoulders.

Put the brown buttercream in an icing bag fitted with a plain nozzle and pipe curly hair on to the clown.

Using the red sugar paste, roll out a large nose and a big mouth, then place them on the cake. Use the green sugar paste to make the small circles for eyes and the circles on the hat. Alternatively, use blue paste for eyes. Add large circles to represent shirt buttons.

ABOUT 20 PORTIONS

NOVELTY BUNS

Illustrated on page 110

Prepare colourful run-outs well in advance of making these cakes. If you prefer, make decorations by stamping shapes out of coloured sugar paste. For very small children, bake the cakes in small paper petits fours cases, and after icing top each with a sugar-coated chocolate bean or other suitable decoration.

double quantity Small Rich Cakes (page 124)
half quantity Quick Fondant (page 31)
food colouring
cut-outs or run-out shapes (pages 75 and 88)

Prepare and bake the cakes following the recipe instructions. Cool the cakes on a wire rack and trim off any tops that have peaked. Make up the fondant and pour a little over each bun until it finds its own level at the top of each paper case. Leave to dry, then decorate each cake with the novelty cut-out or run-out shapes as shown in the photograph on page 110.

ABOUT 20 CAKES

BUILDING BLOCKS

Illustrated on page 111

These individual cakes are ideal for a child's birthday party. The sponge cake can be left plain or it can be split and filled with buttercream or jam if preferred.

Basic Sponge Cake (page 120) baked in a roasting tin
Apricot Glaze (page 20) to coat
1 kg/2¼ lb Sugar Paste (page 42)
4 different food colourings of your choice

Trim the edges of the cake and cut it into 4 cm/1½ inch squares. Brush the pieces of cake with apricot glaze and set aside.

Roll out 100 g/4 oz of the sugar paste thinly. Using small cutters or a fine pointed knife, cut out small letters to decorate the blocks. Re-roll the trimmings and cut out more letters. You will need about 175 letters.

Divide the remaining sugar paste into four and tint each quarter a different colour. Wrap three pieces in cling film and set aside. Roll out the fourth piece thinly and cut it into 10 cm/4 inch squares, re-rolling the scraps as necessary; you will need about eight or nine squares, depending on how many pieces of cake you have cut. Lay a square of the paste over one of the cakes and smooth it down over the corners. Trim off excess paste. Repeat with the remaining paste until all the squares are covered.

Place letters on the blocks, pressing one on each side, then leave to dry for a few hours.

ABOUT 35 BLOCKS

Three-tiered Wedding Cake

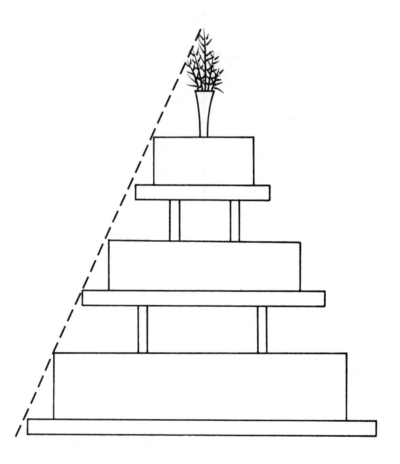

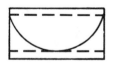 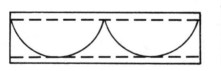 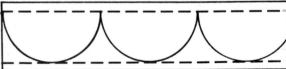

Boy's Christening Cake

Actual size

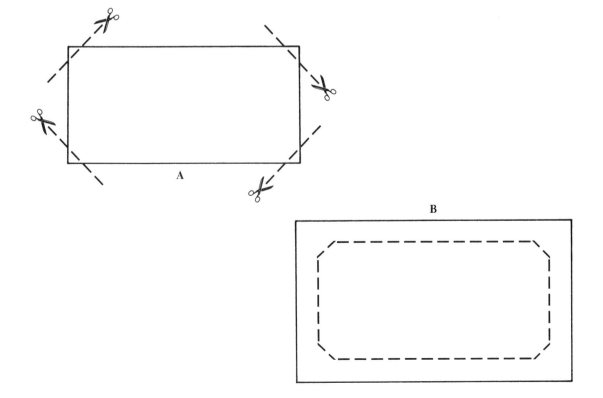

Smoke piped freehand on cake

Couplings piped freehand on cake   Wheels piped freehand on cake

Twenty-first Birthday Cake

A

B

Musical Notes Birthday Cake

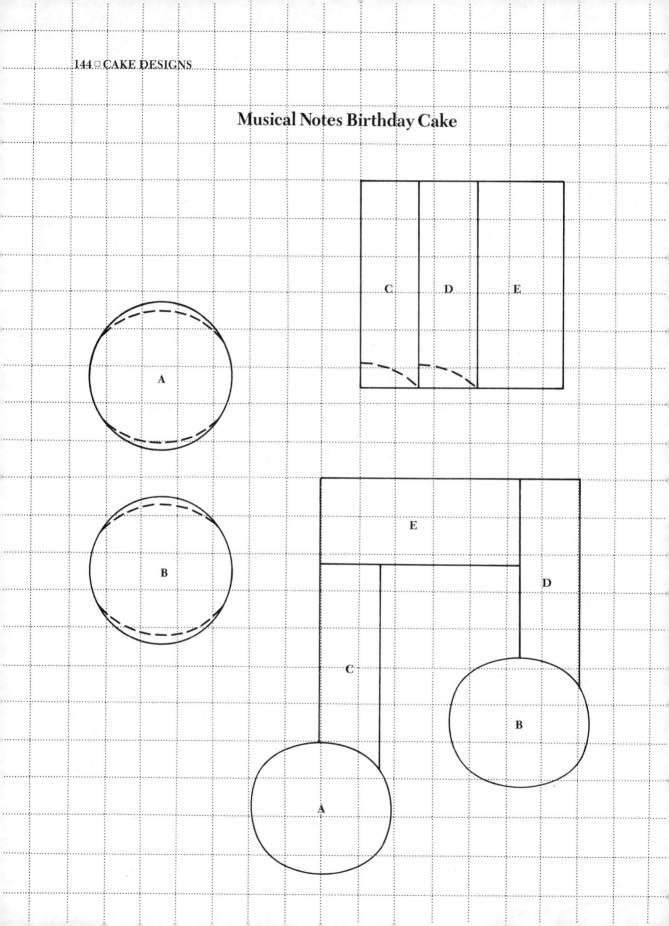

Designs for Brush Embroidery

Harvest Cake

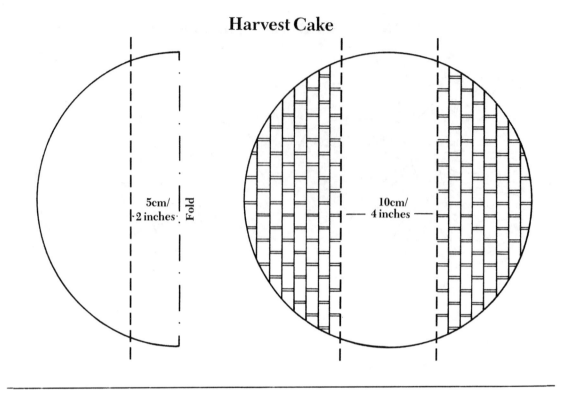

5cm/
2 inches

Fold

10cm/
4 inches

Mini Christmas Cakes

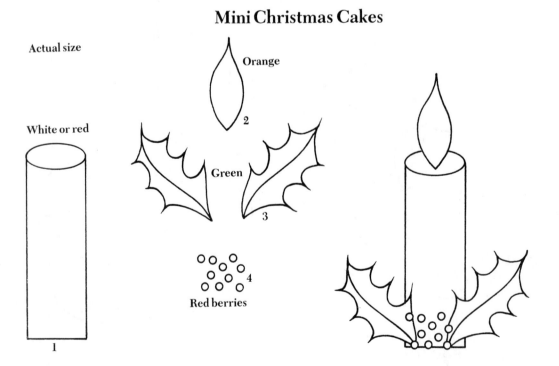

Actual size

White or red

Orange

2

Green

3

Red berries

4

1

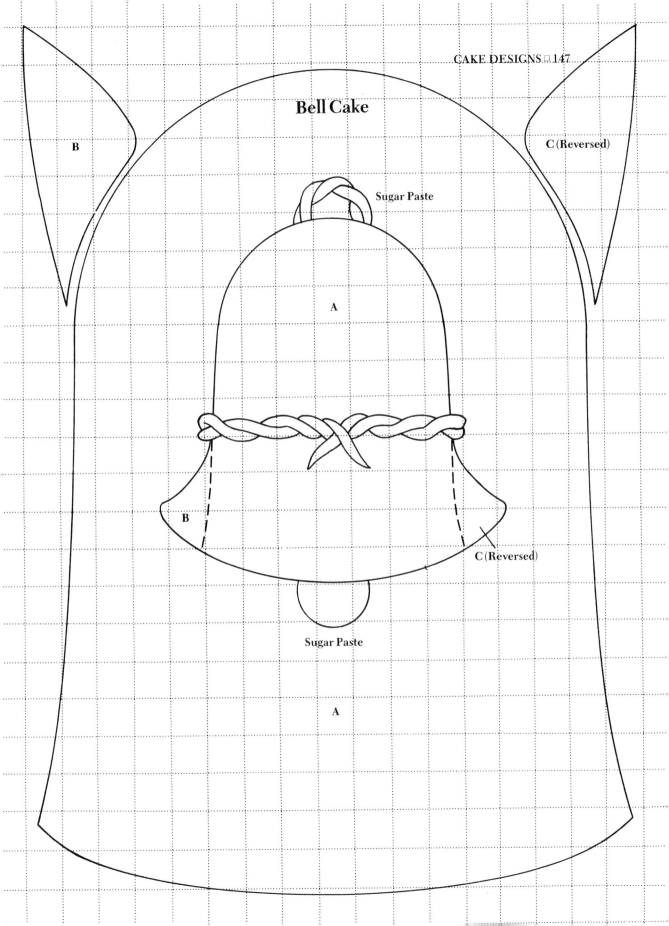

Bell Cake

B

C (Reversed)

Sugar Paste

A

B

C (Reversed)

Sugar Paste

A

Father Christmas Cake

Actual size for Christmas Cake

(Numbers represent order in which to pipe and flood sections).

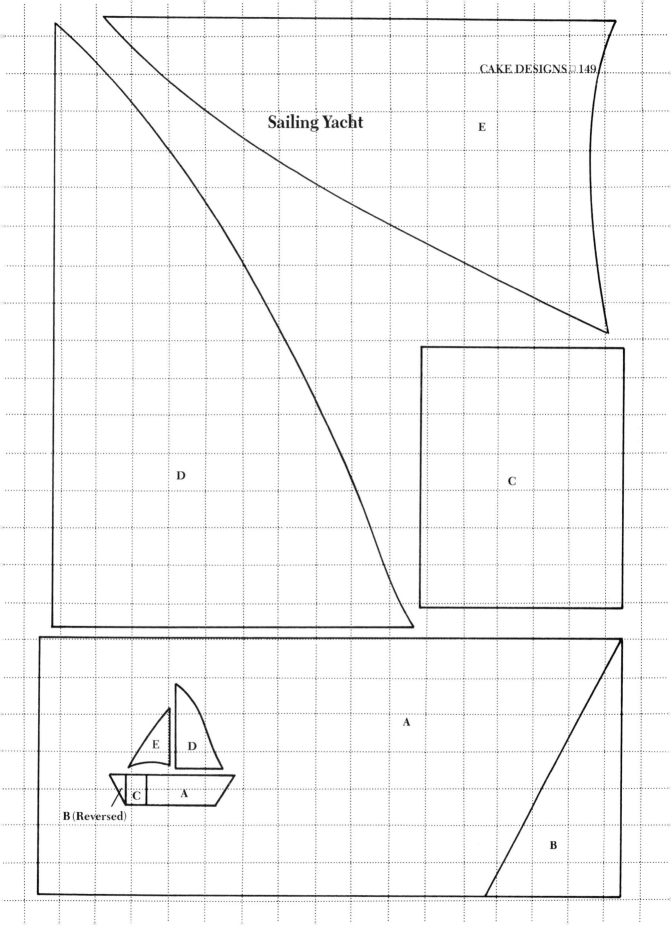

CAKE DESIGNS 149

Sailing Yacht

E

D

C

A

B

B (Reversed)

E   D

C   A

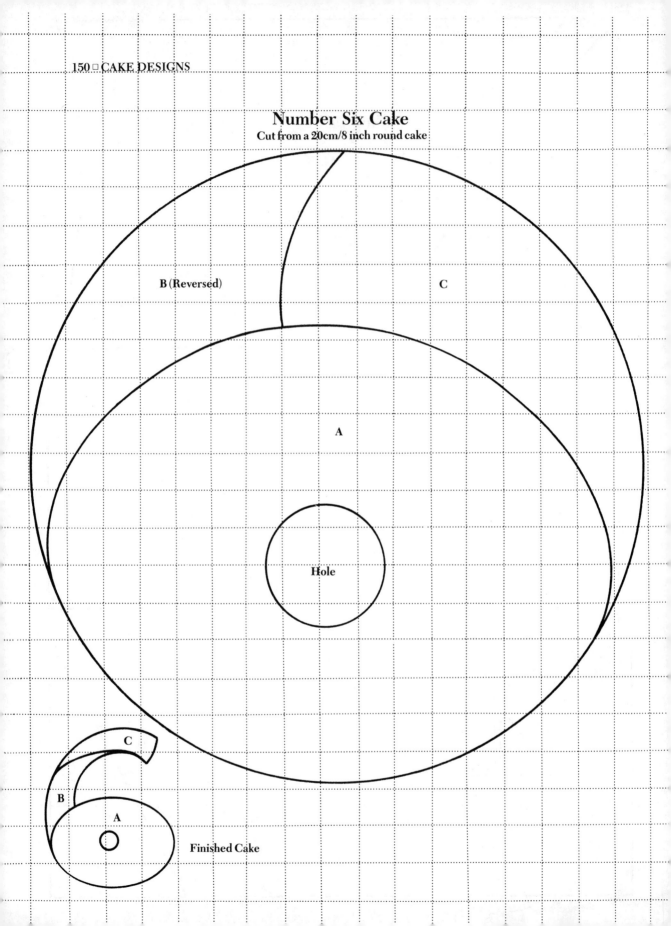

Number Six Cake
Cut from a 20cm/8 inch round cake

B (Reversed)

C

A

Hole

C

B

A

Finished Cake

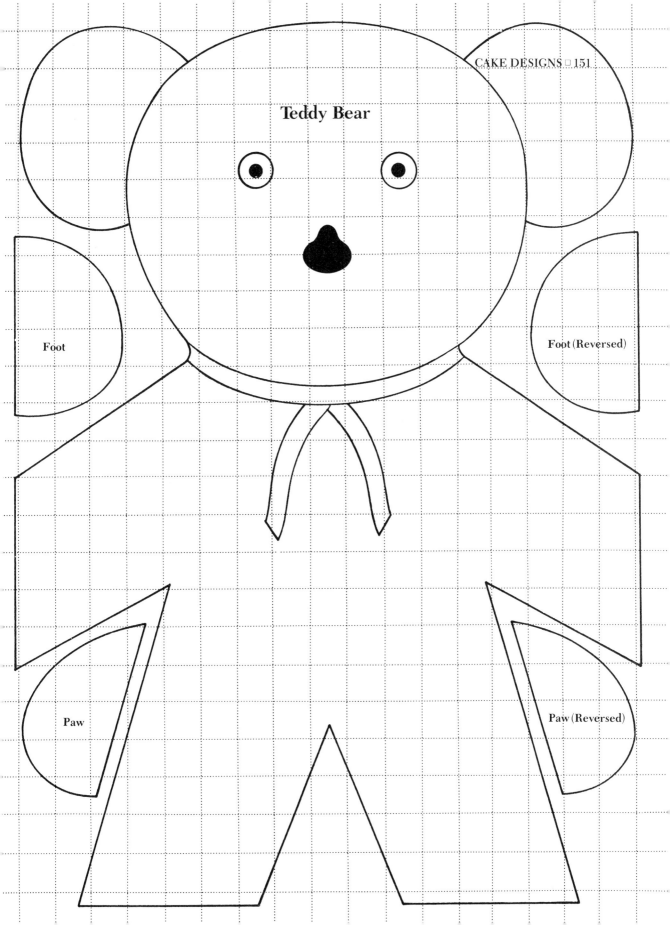

Teddy Bear

Foot

Foot (Reversed)

Paw

Paw (Reversed)

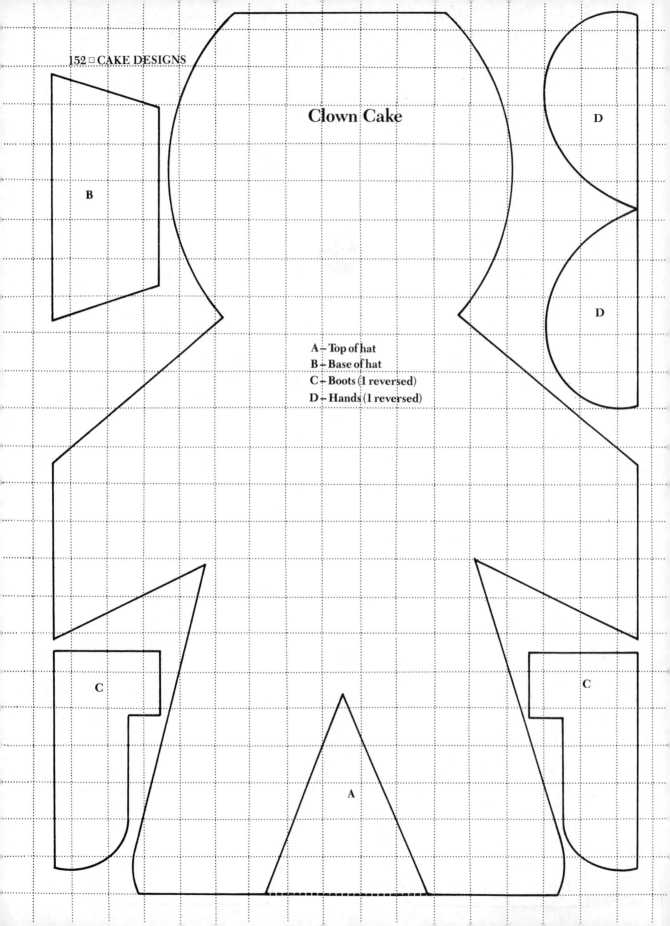

Clown Cake

B

D

D

A – Top of hat
B – Base of hat
C – Boots (1 reversed)
D – Hands (1 reversed)

C

C

A

A B C D E F G H I J K

L M N O P Q R S T U

V W X Y Z a b c d e f g h i

j k l m n o p q r s t u v w x y z

ABCDEFGHIJKLM

NOPQRSTUVWXY

Z 1234567890

ABCDEFGHIJK

LMNOPQRSTU

VWXYZ

HAPPY
BIRTHDAY

MERRY
CHRISTMAS

BEST
WISHES

MOTHERS
DAY

1 2 3 4 5 6

7 8 9 0

1 2 3 4 5 6 7 8 9 0

1 2 3 4 5 6 7 8 9 0

CAKE BOARDS FOR NOVELTY CAKES

Finding a cake board for a large novelty cake can be a problem; however there are alternatives to a shop-bought cake board.

MAKING CAKE BOARDS

Decide on the size and shape of board required and cut out a paper pattern if necessary. For example, you will need a pattern if the board is to be cut in an unusual shape. Square or oblong shapes are the easiest to cover and they usually give the neatest results.

Cut out two or three thicknesses of stiff cardboard from old boxes. Select clean, undamaged card to make a good base. Cover the cardboard and tape the covering neatly in place underneath to hold the carboard layers together securely.

Instead of a cardboard base, a clean chopping board can be covered. For a very large cake, or for a cake that is particularly fragile, a length of laminated shelving can be covered to make a stable base.

COVERING MATERIALS

Cake decorating suppliers often sell the foil covering that is used on commercial cake boards. This is useful for re-covering used cake boards as well as for covering home-made boards. Ordinary cooking foil can be used to cover the boards and a decorative edging can be placed around the board to neaten it. Thick, white baking parchment also makes an attractive board covering for some cakes but a double thickness must be used and the edges should be very neat.

Wrapping papers that have a foil finish are ideal for covering cake boards. Select patterned papers with Christmas motifs or colourful designs to complement the cake. Board edging can be used or buy a length of narrow ribbon which matches the paper

covering and attach it neatly all around the edge of the board.

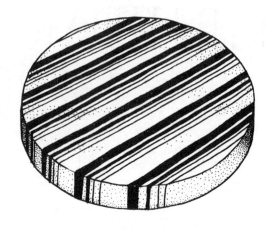

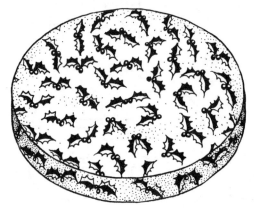

MAKING USE OF OLD CAKE BOARDS

Old cake boards can be re-covered or they can be used as a base on which to make run-outs. The drawn pattern for the run-out can be pinned to the board very successfully, then the completed icing can be left on the board until it has thoroughly dried.

INDEX

Italic page numbers refer to colour photographs; **Bold** page numbers refer to main entries